ZEN
INTERIORS

ZEN INTERIORS

VINNY LEE

Stewart, Tabori & Chang

NEW YORK

DEDICATION

FOR THE SANDMAN

First published in the United States in 1999 by

Stewart, Tabori & Chang

A division of Harry N. Abrams, Inc.

115 West 18th Street

New York, NY 10011

First published in Great Britain in 1999 by Pavilion Books Limited

Picture credits given on page 160

Designed by David Fordham

Library of Congress Cataloging-in-Publication Data
Lee, Vinny
    Zen Interiors / by Vinny Lee.
        p.   cm.
    ISBN 1-55670-930-7 (alk. paper)
    1. Interior decoration--Themes. motives. 2. Zen Buddhism--Influence.
    I. Title.
    NK2113.L44 1999
    747--dc21

Color reproduction by DP Reprographics

Printed and bound in Singapore by Imago

10 9 8 7 6 5 4 3 2

CONTENTS

INTRODUCTION

In these hectic, machine-driven, stressful days of modern living, people are increasingly looking for ways to create havens of calm and relaxation within their own homes. They are searching for an oasis where they can unwind, regain some contact with the natural world, and enjoy a few precious moments of serenity.

This quest for peace and tranquility has led designers and decorators to look to the East to the natural harmony and balance of Asian homes and to the simplicity of their art and design. In this book, *Zen Interiors*, we trace the contemporary influence of the East on the Western home, showing how the calm, natural harmony, and balance that is seen in Asia can be used to create living spaces that provide a tranquil respite from our increasingly frantic lifestyles.

The two main keys to Zen style interiors are simplicity and serenity. These imply the paring down of a cluttered environment and concentration on creating harmony, balance, touch, and texture. By achieving these things you can create a place where the spiritual or inner needs can be addressed and where you can indulge in calming or stimulating the senses with light, space, and a free flow of energy.

Among the beliefs of Zen is the conviction that you can find pleasure in even the most simple of everyday tasks—in bathing, meditation, and preparation of food—so the rooms or spaces where these activities take place are important. Eating Places, Living Rooms, Sleeping Spaces, and Water Rooms are each individual areas that should be arranged and decorated to create tranquil and calming atmospheres.

Place simple objects within these rooms and they will be a source of enjoyment and wonder. Against a plain white wall, the color and shape of a single stem of a perfect flower will become a feature, a fish swimming in a pond or water tumbling over a stone can become mesmeric and absorbing. Take inspiration, too, from Zen haiku poetry as these poems feature many natural elements. Choose earthy or basic objects that are not only decorative but also provide a way of keeping in touch with the natural world. Use plants such as

The clean lines of this kitchen space make it appear to be more than just a workroom. The use of color and steel against a white background emphasize the shapes of the worktop, cupboards, and stools.

Z

bamboo, a small arrangement of rounded pebbles collected from the beach or an uninterrupted flow of air through open windows dressed with translucent drapes. Each reveal nature and its intrinsic beauty.

Balance is another important feature of Zen life and lifestyle, and achieving the right balance will lead to harmony and tranquility. So, an active, busy city life should be counteracted by tranquil time spent at home or in the country; dark areas in a room should be balanced by light, and rough textures offset by smooth. In Zen terms, the two areas in life that weight against or with each other are referred to as yin and yang, which can also be interpreted as male and female or positive and negative.

Essentially, the Zen home is about less is more, that a few well chosen pieces are more worthwhile than a pile of clutter. Zen thinking follows the idea that a person can become weighed down and burdened with possessions and that to gain freedom of spirit, possessions should be rationalized and limited.

The use of minimalism, purity of form, function, and shape is important in this Asian style of interior, but it is not a new approach. These are factors that have appealed to countless leading architects and designers around the world. In the early part of the century, the German architect Mies van der Rohe coined the phrase, "Less is More"; in the 1930s, the Finnish designer Alvar Aalto took the marriage of form and function to new heights, and one of today's most acclaimed architects, London-based John Pawson (who himself spent several years teaching in Japan), has made the pared down environment an architectural art form.

Zen style does not have to be an all or nothing change, it is something you can take in your own time, changing a little here and there and maintaining an environment you feel comfortable with. Take inspiration from restrained, uncluttered rooms in which the proportions, space and light create the decoration and start by trying to make one room a place of utmost purity and calm. In turn, this may lead to the transformation of others in your home.

In this book we look at Zen style interiors, how the pure Zen approach can be adapted and tailored to suit not only the Western climate and way of life but also to our buildings and settings, whether they be a red brick Victorian terraced house, a barn in the country, or an inner city apartment.

The light at the end of the corridor not only attracts attention, it also promises a journey and hints and interest beyond. The angular-like nature of the wall and corridor create a feeling of height and space.

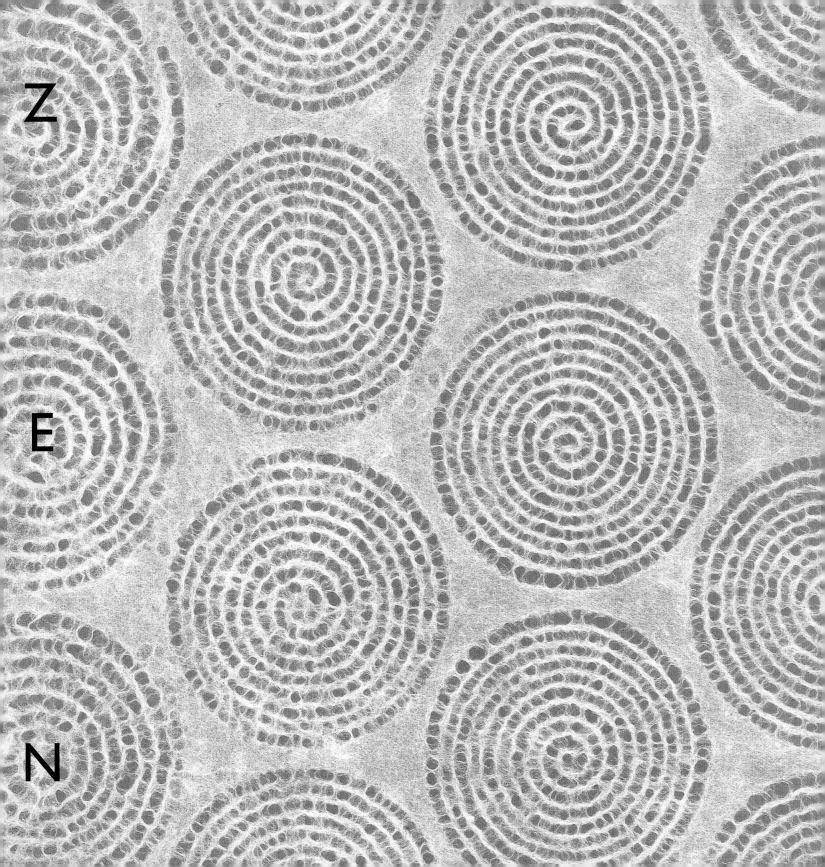

PART ONE
INSPIRATION

SIMPLICITY

SIMPLICITY AND SERENITY HAVE LONG BEEN ASSOCIATED WITH THE LIFESTYLES AND HABITS OF MANY RELIGIOUS GROUPS AND WORSHIPPERS, BOTH IN THE EAST AND WEST. ZEN CAN BE SEEN, TOO, IN MANY WAYS OF LIFE IN AISA. THESE RANGE FROM THE SPARTAN FURNISHINGS OF MONKS' AND NUNS' CELLS TO THE ECONOMY AND CRAFTSMANSHIP OF THE SHAKERS' FURNISHINGS AND THE BASIC AND UNADORNED REQUIREMENTS OF THE PURITANS AND AMISH.

IN MANY SCHOOLS OF THOUGHT, CLEANLINESS AND SERENITY ARE CLOSELY LINKED. CLEANLINESS IS SAID TO BE NEXT TO GODLINESS, AND ORDER AND DISCIPLINE ARE THE BACKBONE OF MOST DOCTRINES. IN SOME CASES, THESE IDEAS ARE TAKEN TO EXTREMES BUT AS A BASIC PRINCIPLE THEY ARE GOOD GUIDELINES. CLEANLINESS CAN BE INTERPRETED IN MANY WAYS FROM BEING NEAT, ORDERED, AND METHODICAL TO PURE IN THOUGHT AND MIND. CLEANLINESS, AS IN HYGIENE, IS NOT ONLY BENEFICIAL FOR HEALTH AND APPEARANCE BUT THE SIMPLE ACT OF BATHING CAN IN ITSELF BE CALMING AND MEDITATIVE, AS CAN THE EFFECT OF CLEANSING YOUR HOME OR ENVIRONMENT OF UNNECESSARY CLUTTER AND POSSESSIONS.

SIMPLICITY IN INTERIOR STYLE IS NOT NECESSARILY HARD, COLD, AND MINIMAL, AND SERENITY IS NOT JUST A MYSTICAL CONCEPT. THROUGH APPLICATION, BOTH ARE ATTAINABLE AND CAN BE ACHIEVED AT DIFFERENT LEVELS. THE TRICK IS TO FIND THE LEVEL THAT SUITS YOU THE BEST—THE ONE THAT YOU ARE AT EASE WITH AND THE ONE THAT GIVES YOU THE MOST COMFORT.

The simplicity of this arrangement makes the mind and eye study it in detail; if there was a group of objects they would distract from each other and cause confusion.

& SERENITY

Even when a fire is not burning, the hearth can be made to look interesting and inviting by arranging a pile of logs, pine cones, or even stones to fill the void.

If you are unsettled in surroundings devoid of color and decoration, or have to strive too hard to keep your room immaculately tidy, then don't go against your nature as it will only bring stress and anxiety. Instead, try to find a balance where there is order within your capabilities and daily routine—but not a rigid regime—so that you are not adding to the burdens of an already busy lifestyle.

THE WIDER PERSPECTIVE

When it comes to creating a simple and serene environment, begin at the outer edges and work in, so that everything around you is conducive to a calm state. This, in turn, will have the same effect upon you. It is also easier and more logical to start with the larger aspects of a room, such as walls and floors, and work in to the smaller items and details. The features that you should especially concentrate and expand on are the windows (especially if the view is attractive), and other light sources and openings. But above all, see just how much quietness and serenity you can achieve within the space. Serenity is

Using simple bands of color and shape to delineate uses can be effective. For example, the area on either side of the fireplace has been painted in a copper-like color that highlights the warmth of the fire.

most likely to come about through simplicity in your surroundings and, as with the Zen principles of balance, this should be through contact with nature and light.

As a starting point, a perfect, plain-walled shell of a room is not always possible. There may be ornate cornices, pipes, radiators, beams, fireplaces, or other architectural features that are *in situ* and impossible or financially inhibiting to remove. So, to create the most basic and clear aspect to the room, conceal, disguise, or decorate these intrusions to blend with the overall color and finish. They should be disguised in as unobtrusive a way as possible so as not to distract the eye or inhibit the free-flowing arrangement of furniture and furnishings within.

Boxing-in pipes and ugly radiators can be done cheaply with plywood or other similar lightweight material, but make sure that the cover does not touch the heat source directly as it may scorch or discolor. With radiators it is worth installing a grille or cutting a simple open pattern into the front panel of the cover so that the heat can travel into the room. Putting in false walls or panels can be expensive,

but a drape of fabric or a light curtain can be easily fixed in front of an ugly feature and create a simple but effective distraction.

Keep wall colors pale to reflect what natural light is available, but the walls don't necessarily have to be white. Warmer tones of cream are often better in colder northern locations, where daylight hours are shorter in the winter and the strength of light is dulled by clouds or weather. A hint of warmth in shades of cream or yellow gives an impression of sun and comfort, which is relaxing and therefore calming. To create a less brilliant and harsh setting that is also restful and inviting, use tints of natural shades such as oatmeal, browns, muted greens and grays.

In warmer climates, or rooms used during the summer, pure white and soft hues of sky blue, almond green or lemon are refreshing and cooling. With white it may be necessary to add voile blinds to the windows to prevent glare from sunlight, which can be very difficult for the eyes to cope with and causes headaches and neck pains.

You may also want to choose colors to suit the use of the room. Think of blue for cleansing and washing as well as tranquility, and

Bringing elements of the outside into the home can help to keep you in touch with nature and the seasons. This small shrub can be moved outdoors in the summer to benefit from the rain and sun but kept indoors when frost and winter weather may damage it.

perhaps the palest wash of terracotta or a blush of pink or lavender for a calming, restful bedroom. With true Zen interiors, the colors are simple, plain, and light rather than heavy and dense.

Although carpet may be useful for sound insulation in an apartment and for comfort underfoot, the most understated and simple floors are generally wood, stone, or rush matting. Matting such as tatami, coir, seagrass, or sisal has a similar softness and the same sound dampening facilities as carpet. In addition, it also has the earthy, natural, and aesthetic appearance that is equated with a Zen interior. Such hard floorings as stone, slate, marble, and terracotta are cool underfoot but are ideal for areas such as hallways, bathrooms, and kitchens. In these particular rooms, water and wear and tear take their toll on natural fiber floor coverings.

In areas where food is prepared or eaten, these smooth, easy to brush surfaces have the advantage that when food or crumbs are spilt on the surface they are quick and easy to remove. With matting, the food may become lodged in the weave and stain the plain, pale colored finish.

RIGHT: This wood floor, which runs through from the hall to the dining area, is easy to maintain, is a natural material, and also give the impression of unity between the two rooms.

A single bowl of fruit becomes an object of interest in monotone surroundings and where the angular shapes of the walls are played off against the cylindrical pillar. The horizontal opening where the bowl is placed frames the object making it appear like a picture in a long frame.

PARING DOWN

Simplicity in your selection of furnishings, objects, and color enhances a room's sense of space and calmness and a few well chosen *objets d'art* give more pleasure and a clearer image than stacks of things piled on top of and in front of each other. Try to edit your possessions. Eliminate clutter, throw away stacks of newspapers and magazines that you will never get round to reading, and sort out that shoe box that is full of photographs.

If you tend to cover your sofa with piles of cushions, ask yourself if you really need them all. Are they required for support or are they for decoration? If they are for support, perhaps what you really need is a new sofa. But if they are purely decorative, ask yourself would two or three specifically chosen cushions not be more attractive than a jumble, which invariably ends up on the floor?

Shape is also an important factor in Zen philosophy. A row of clear white pottery urns or vases are not in themselves eye-catching because their color is uniform and plain, but because the eye is not distracted by elaborate paintwork, the pure shape of the object

becomes the focal point. Shadows can also play an important part in turning a plain object into something special. If the object is positioned so that a shadow is cast to one side, the three-dimensional effect of the object or frame is exaggerated. This simple use of light can be very effective in a number of ways and is discussed at more length in Light and Natural on pages 60–7.

Simplicity of form and decoration also means that the material from which the object is made takes on a prime role. For example, in a white room, a plain wooden shelf or sill becomes prominent because it lies across the upright lines in the rest of the room and it has an element of color. With this concentration of focus it is important that the wood is of good quality and a high finish. It should also preferably have a textural, grainy finish such as that on a piece of driftwood. The Shaker motto "Hearts to God and Hands to Work" was a belief that they followed when creating their simple but exquisitely made furniture. The Shakers believed that God was omnipresent and could see everywhere so that even the inside back of a drawer, concealed in a cabinet or cupboard, must be as perfect as the front, because He would be able to see it. Shaker furniture may be simply styled but it has elegance and serenity.

The importance of quality applies to all decorative objects and as a question of economics it means that in the Zen interior, you only need buy one, beautifully made item of quality instead of a number or group of inferior or fussy pieces.

Ikebana—the Zen form of flower arranging—is another example of paring down. Instead of a bunch of mixed flowers arranged in a vase, ikebana uses a single, elegant stem or spray of bloom and in some cases a branch of twisted willow. In ikebana, the contrast of the curling wood and the delicate bloom is considered to be the perfect balance of yin and yang and the eye is drawn to it to appreciate the beauty of the single bloom rather than the overall effect of a mixed or large bunch of flowers.

The philosophy of clearing your surroundings and hence your mind is one that works for most people. With fewer things to tidy and less dusting to worry about, you have peace of mind and more freedom to enjoy other things. Less furniture and decoration also means that a room is brighter, clearer, and more composed. This, in turn, gives the impression of tranquility.

HARMONY

ONCE THE SIMPLE, BASIC STRUCTURE AND DECORATION OF THE ROOM HAS BEEN ACHIEVED, THE NEXT STAGE IS TO ADD THE FURNISHINGS AND OBJECTS. THE WAY THAT THESE ITEMS ARE PLACED AND ARRANGED DEFINES THE BALANCE OF THE OVERALL SCHEME AND CAN BE USED TO COMPENSATE FOR ANY IMBALANCES.

AS WITH CHORDS IN MUSIC, ACHIEVE HARMONY IN COLOR BY USING TONES FROM THE SAME FAMILY. A TOO SHARP CONTRAST OR CLASH CREATES DISCORD, WHICH JARS OR AGGRAVATES, RATHER THAN RELAXES, THE MIND. THE THREE PRIMARY COLORS ARE RED, BLUE AND YELLOW. COLORS THAT WORK TOGETHER WELL ARE THOSE WITHIN THE FAMILIES THAT ARE MADE BY BLENDING THESE COLORS. FOR EXAMPLE, RED, BLUE, AND PURPLE ARE ONE FAMILY—PURPLE BEING THE COLOR MADE BY COMBINING RED AND BLUE. YELLOW, RED, AND ORANGE ARE A SIMILAR PARENT AND OFFSPRING GROUP, AND BLUE, YELLOW, AND GREEN ARE THE FINAL FAMILY. BY KEEPING WITHIN THE FAMILY GROUPS OR USING SHADES OF A SINGLE COLOR, THE SCHEME WILL BE HARMONIOUS.

ALSO PLAY WITH COLOR USING CONTRASTING SHADES AS REPRESENTED BY THE YIN AND YANG SYMBOL WHERE ONE HALF IS BLACK AND THE OTHER WHITE. BY USING COLORS THAT HAVE DIFFERENT STRENGTHS IT IS POSSIBLE TO DEVISE AREAS OF DIFFERENT MOOD WITHIN THE SAME ROOM, OR A SINGLE EYE-CATCHING FEATURE. THE COLORS DON'T HAVE TO BE DIAMETRICALLY OPPOSITE LIKE BLACK AND WHITE, THEY CAN BE EXTREMES OF DARK AND LIGHT WITHIN THE SAME COLOR. FOR EXAMPLE, PALEST POWDER BLUE AND MIDNIGHT BLUE, A BLUSH OF PINK AND DEEP VERMILION. THE COLORS ARE LINKED BY BEING FROM A COMMON PALETTE BUT OPPOSITE IN RESPECT OF STRENGTH AND EFFECT.

By creating a recess in the wall it is possible to display a three-dimensional object but keep it flush, rather than proud, with the wall surface. This sort of display area is ideal in a hallway as the object will be safely tucked away from the accidental brushes or knocks of passing traffic.

& BALANCE

LEFT: This raised platform creates a break in the through flow of space from one area to another and provides a place of rest and tranquility. Avoid the temptation to overdress such a platform: keep the furniture simple and appropriate.

RIGHT: A row of identical ribbed pots planted with cacti makes an interesting feature between two cupboards. The simple pots in identical color and style allow the shapes of the cacti to be the focal point.

In the world of Zen philosophy, the balance of elements and nature is central to its beliefs and so vital to the Zen interior, implemented through color as well as objects. Earth and water, fire and forest elements should be represented in equal proportions, and where an element is missing or insufficiently represented, use color to redress the equilibrium.

For example, if it is not feasible to have water in a room, use a blue silk cushion or a turquoise vase or bowl to represent the feature. Fire can be easily mimicked by a candle but then again a small, polished brass or copper dish appears fiery and of similar hues. To represent earth, use small rounded pebbles, or sand simply poured into a shallow bowl—the act of letting grains of sand run through your fingers can also be very calming. Wood or terracotta flooring is another good way of bringing this element into a room.

Shapes, too, are important. Zen considers straight lines to be more restful than curves because they suggest calmness, but it is also against the rigidity of exactness and parallels because they are not true to nature. Zen symbols include the "living" circle, which is drawn freehand and deliberately slightly untrue to suggest that it is a form of nature rather than one made by machine. So once again, a balance is found between lines and curves.

USING FURNITURE FOR BALANCE

In a room where there is a fireplace chimney intruding into the space, redress the balance by painting a compatible and comparable size of dark area on the wall opposite, which will give the impression that the area is deeper or set back. In this way, a yin and yang balance of opposites is created. Or add a cabinet or something of a similar size, which will mirror the shape and so be equally harmonious. Apply a similar remedy to a recess or archway.

In small rooms or rooms where there are a number of irregular features, use movable screens to give a lightweight and non-permanent balance to architectural features. Place a screen to complement a lone or irregular feature or use it to shield or hide part of a large or unwieldy form. The screen should be simple and unobtrusive so that it does not become a feature in its own right. Typical Japanese screens are made of natural wood frames filled with plain white opaque paper, or simple fabrics or fine matting may be used.

When arranging furniture you should also aim to achieve symmetry. For example, if you have two sofas in a room they should be the same size and placed facing each other. Or balance one sofa with two armchairs that together have a similar volume. A dining table and chairs will be more pleasing to the eye if there are the same number of identical chairs on either side of the table.

Traditionally, there is little furniture in the Zen dwelling. The main pieces are futon-type mattresses or rolls and legless chairs (to support the back of a person sitting cross-legged or at a low table for a tea ceremony) and a couple of chests for possessions and clothing. They are often arranged around the edge of the room to leave ample floor space for sitting or lying in the center. Ensure hard and soft surfaces are incorporated in equal quantities. Offset a hard floor such as slate and a glass-topped table with soft woollen throws draped on upholstered easy chairs. A couple of floor cushions will further redress the balance. These guidelines are also just practical design rules in that too many hard corners are uncomfortable to live with as

they can be bruising to bump into, and too many angles pointing in and out of the room, like arrow heads, may feel threatening and unsettling.

BALANCING LIGHT AND SHADE

Areas of light and shade should be similarly balanced. A room needs to have aspects of both. Light is necessary to invigorate and brighten the space, but areas of shade are equally important for relaxation and contemplation. The natural light within a room will alter during the day resulting in changing areas of brightness and shadow. So when you are deciding on the positions of heavier items of furniture take into consideration when and how you will want to use them and how they will affect the distribution of light.

If the overall scheme of your room is neutral, you may like to change the dressings to complement or reflect the time of year. For example, a throw and cushions and even the curtains can be changed to give a fresh and appropriate look to the room every four months

The louver blinds at the window allow the strength and direction of light to be easily adjusted to suit the mood and activity taking place in the room. The slats can also be closed to provide a view or to create total privacy within.

During the spring and summer you may want to leave the windows uncovered so that you can enjoy the view and benefit from the natural daylight. If this is the case, winter curtains can be taken down, cleaned, and stored until they are next needed.

or so. If you have a fine voile curtain to screen the view and another, heavier curtain for added warmth in winter you can vary the combination of curtains. For example, in winter you would use both together, in the spring and autumn, you may keep the heavier curtains drawn back and tied to frame the window and leave the voile closed. Then in summer, the heavier curtains could be removed and the light, voile curtain left to frame the window.

NATURAL HARMONY

Take the balance of the seasons into consideration in your interior. To keep in touch with nature it can be therapeutic to create a small cameo or point of interest that highlights the time of year. For example, in spring, a tray of wheat grass or a pot of seasonal bulbs growing bright and green reinforces the feeling of renewal. In summer, a bunch of scented herbs such as basil, thyme, lemon balm, or rosemary that has been bought from the market or picked from the garden, acts in the same way.

By scenting the air you can enhance your feeling of well-being. You may choose the perfume to suit your mood or to complement the season, for example lavender for a calming ambience or citrus or lily of the valley fragrances to emulate the scent of spring.

These herbs are not for drying. Keep them planted or in water as they suggest a balance between the outer and inner worlds of the garden and the home. In the fall, a simple arrangement of crisp golden leaves, a bowl of glossy red apples, or shining brown horse chestnuts can be a focus, and in the winter, a graceful, leafless branch, a single snowy white flower, or a pine cone.

Also use plants and water together to reduce pollution and noise by creating a barrier or forming a close point of interest. By placing a window box of plants on a sill or a screen of plants at one side of a desk or chair you can make an intrusive noise seem more distant and less immediate.

It is good to make use of water by itself in office environments and warmer rooms in the house. It will evaporate and add moisture to the air, so helping to counteract the dryness and stuffiness that is all too readily created by machines such as computers, faxes, and phones. The same applies at home where the television and hi-fi system can cause the air to become dehydrated. By adding these elements of water you will also achieve a greater harmony between machines and nature.

As well as stimulating your visual pleasure with arrangements of carefully chosen objects, add to the harmony of your environment by using scent to create a balance between the arousal of the senses of sight and smell. Oils and burners will perfume the air and waft through a whole room. Alternatively, be more specific by putting dried citrus peel, lavender bags, or sandalwood into a drawer or cupboard. Scented candles are also very popular and can be used in most rooms to create an inviting atmosphere. By carefully floating candles in a bowl of water, an unusual combination of elements is created that is both calming and soothing.

Fragrances should be balanced and harmonious so try to choose the scent that most suits your moods or the room you are in. Some scents are uplifting and stimulating while others are soothing and relaxing. Do not use too many scents: a mix of floral rose candles, citrus lemon room-scenter, and nutmeg and clove potpourri will be overpowering and clawing. Instead, pick one theme—such as floral—and use, say, the rose candles with perhaps just a hint of lavender perfume emitting from a bowl or bunch of dried flowers.

TOUCH

LEFT: The grain of wood has its own unique pattern that can be highlighted when sanded smooth and waxed, sealed, or varnished. Wood also comes in infinite shades and colors from the black of ebony to the pale, silvery tones of limed oak.

SENSING STIMULI ARE ALL OVER THE BODY AND ANY AREA OF THE SKIN THAT COMES IN CONTACT WITH A MATERIAL OR SUBSTANCE WILL SENSE AND FEEL IT. EVEN WITH YOUR EYES CLOSED, SO CUTTING OFF THE VISUAL RECEPTORS, YOU CAN TOUCH AND HANDLE THE TEXTURE OR FORM OF AN OBJECT OR FABRIC AND GIVE AN ACCURATE DESCRIPTION OF WHAT IT IS—AS THOUGH YOUR FINGERS WERE DOING THE SEEING.

IN THE SIMPLE SURROUNDINGS OF THE ZEN INTERIOR, TOUCH AND TEXTURE BECOME MAJOR PLAYERS. IN THE ROOM THAT HAS BEEN PAIRED DOWN AND EDITED, THE FEW ITEMS THAT ARE LEFT BECOME VITAL COMPONENTS IN THE OVERALL APPEARANCE AND SO THE EYE, AND OFTEN THE HAND, WILL BE DRAWN TO THEM. A SINGLE VELVET CUSHION ON A ROUGHLY TEXTURED, LINEN-COVERED SOFA; A COOL, CLEAR GLASS BOWL ON A RICH CHENILLE CLOTH; A PRICKLY PINE CONE ON A SILKY SOFT MAT; A SOFT WOOLLEN THROW CASUALLY DRAPED OVER THE BACK OF A SMOOTH LEATHER CHAIR—EACH TEMPTS YOU TO FEEL THEM, TO COME IN CLOSER CONTACT WITH THE OBJECT.

THINK OF THE EFFECT OF THESE MATERIALS WHEN TOUCHED. IMAGINE A COOL, SMOOTH STONE FLOOR UNDER YOUR FEET ON A HOT SUMMER'S DAY; A WARM, COMFORTABLE BRUSHED WOOL BLANKET AROUND YOUR SHOULDERS ON A COOL EVENING, AND A CRISP, LAUNDERED LINEN PILLOWCASE NEXT TO YOUR CHEEK. THE SENSE OF TOUCH AFFECTS ALL PARTS OF THE BODY AND PLAYS AN IMPORTANT ROLE IN EACH ROOM OF YOUR HOME. BY PLACING THE RIGHT MATERIALS AND OBJECTS IN THE APPROPRIATE LOCATION YOU CAN CREATE SIMPLE, OFTEN UNCONSCIOUS, PLEASURE AND ENJOYMENT.

& TEXTURE

ABOVE: Although smooth surfaces are pleasant to run your fingers over, rough ones can be interesting and stimulating. Stone, such as pumice, can be used decoratively or practically, as an abrasive scrub for rough skin.

On a larger scale, use the juxtaposition of hard and soft textures to highlight a space in dramatic ways. Smooth plaster beside an area of exposed rough brick makes the level area appear even more regular and the brick more rugged. In the same way, the unbroken regularity of a polished marble table top laid with roughly woven jute mats, or a stone bathroom floor with a luxurious, fluffy, soft toweling mat are contrasts that are most appealing. Furthermore, they attract not only the sense of touch but also sight. The visual play of textures and finishes can be stimulating.

TEXTURAL SOFT FURNISHINGS

Textures can be cold and warm to the touch, and sometimes the same material can have both effects. Smooth silky fabrics tend to be sensual and luxurious, but a fiber such as silk can also be both warm and cool when worn or in close contact with the skin. In a hot climate, silk is cool because it is a natural material and allows moisture and perspiration to escape, but in the cold it insulates and maintains the body's natural heat. It is also a light and durable fabric, so easy to wear and live with as well as being long-lasting.

Linen and cotton have similarly diverse properties. Cotton can be finely woven and cool yet when the surface is brushed to a light pile, as in brushed cotton sheets, it becomes warm and comforting. Linen can be as smooth as fine sheets, as rough as hopsack-style curtains, or excitingly textured like fibrous towels that are used to invigorate the skin when drying.

Man-made materials are now so sophisticated that many copy or closely imitate the original or natural versions, but they have been developed so as not to have the disadvantages that are seen, by some, to be a problem with the "real" thing. For example, crease-resistant and stain-repellent fabrics and finishes mean that it is now possible to have the white or the palest of covers on furniture in a family home. Dog paw marks, sticky, chocolatey fingers, and the odd drip of red wine are no longer the horror they used to be. Flammable materials are now treated to be flame-retardant, absorbent ones to be waterproof, and there is machine-washable, non-shrink wool, which means that even the most precious wool blankets and covers can be chucked in the washing machine without remorse.

The soft folds and textural surface of the throw on the sofa are in contrast to the polished stone blocks that are used as tables. Both the wool throw and the stone blocks are tactile and inviting in different ways—the throw because it is soft and warm and the stone for its smooth, cool surface. These contrasts add interest in a room.

Wood pulp and plant cellulose are also used as a basis for man-made materials. Although the base component is natural, the manufacturing process remolds and reforms the fibers to have greater potential for manufacturing. Even some of the most synthetic fabrics have been developed to have "breathable" properties and with man-made fibers, the possibilities for creating textures and finishes is infinite as the fibers can be formed and chemically adjusted to achieve the look desired.

The texture of a fabric also affects the way it drapes and folds and therefore has some influence on where it is positioned. Long lengths of material, such as curtains and drapes, are generally required to have a comparatively soft handle or feel, because they will be required to fold back on themselves when drawn away from a window. Stiff fabrics, such as treated nylon or materials with a metallic finish, can be used to great effect, but they will fold back in angular columns rather than graceful folds. Heavy fabrics, such as velvet or rich brocades, fall into a few, larger, more rounded folds, whereas the finer muslins and gauzes concertina into many tiny pencil pleats.

LEFT: The check pattern, as well as the size and shape of the cushions on the bed highlight the squares of wood panelling used to create the screen, which acts as a headboard.

RIGHT: Simple banners of cream cotton calico are used to break up the background wall covering of plain barlap. The banners can easily be removed for washing or to be replaced by another color or pattern of banner for a different occasion or seasonal change.

So, when choosing a material for a curtain take into consideration the effect of having a heavy curtain around a window. It will not fold so much when drawn back so it will restrict the amount of light that comes into the room by narrowing the size of the window. This can be an advantage in a room with a number of large windows, but where there is a single small window it could be detrimental, preventing daylight from entering.

Soft fabrics can also be used like sculpture to create rounded edges around hard, angular features and to take the sharpness away from boxy furniture. The throw has become one of the most useful and versatile pieces of cloth in interior decorating. It can be used for numerous purposes from a tablecloth to a shawl to wrap around your shoulders. In many cases, throws are used over chairs and sofas to break up the size of a large piece or to cover worn and marked material underneath. By using a throw in a contrasting shade to the background of the upholstered furniture, it reduces the overall size. The same effect is created by using a patterned throw on a plain background or vice versa.

RIGHT: Although this metal and wood staircase is sturdy and robust it appears to be lightweight and delicate because the treads have been left open, which allows daylight to pass through easily from one level to another.

RIGHT: The rough unfinished texture of the handrails echoes the thick wooden treads of the stairs. This rough, chunkiness gives a feeling of permanence and stability.

In the Zen interior, the illusion of space and the flow of the air around is of vital importance. Where there are a number of doors opening in and out of a room, making it feel like a thoroughfare, use a panel of fine fabric instead of a solid door. A small room can also be made to feel more spacious if the door is replaced by a voile or opaque sheer hanging. Light shines through from a hallway or passage beyond, giving the illusion of space. Opening up a room like this is also good for the circulation of air and ventilation.

HARDER TEXTURAL SURFACES

As well as linen, wool, cotton, and silk, there are many other natural materials that can be used in the home to enhance the Zen-like qualities of an interior. Wood, reed, bamboo, seagrass, coir, and cork can be employed in numerous ways and all have textures that add to the complexity and interest of a scheme. Wood is probably one of the most versatile materials known to man, it is used to build the structure of a home as well as to decorate it with the finest turned

bowls and slim-slatted blinds. The textures and colors of wood are many, from the blackness of dark walnut to the richness of mahogany and paleness of scrubbed oak, pine, or birch. Wood can also be stained, bleached, limed and painted, glazed, lacquered and sanded to a matt but smooth finish.

Seagrass, coir, and reed are all used in floor coverings and again can be woven from a smooth, silky finish to deep, waffle-effect cells with loose fibers. These floor coverings are a popular natural finish for a room; they have sound absorbent qualities similar to carpet and a softness underfoot unlike stone and wood floors. However, maintenance of this type of flooring needs to be done carefully and regularly. Some floors require to be watered to keep the fibers from breaking and splitting and most require regular and efficient vacuum cleaning, especially in areas where food is eaten or prepared. Crumbs and bits of food can be ground into the matting and may eventually go moldy or rot. It is also worth checking on the finish of the flooring when you buy it; if it is untreated, the pale, natural color may darken and be prone to staining.

SEEING

IN KEEPING WITH THE ZEN IDEAL OF BEING IN TOUCH WITH NATURE, THE PERFECT ZEN HOME WOULD HAVE LARGE SLIDING DOORS AND GENEROUS WINDOWS THAT LOOK OUT OVER A GARDEN WITH A GOLDFISH POND, WEEPING WILLOWS, SHRUBS, FLOWERS, AND SCULPTURAL STONES. THE GARDEN WOULD BE CAREFULLY PLANNED TO ALLOW FOR A BALANCE OF YIN AND YANG AND, FOR THE PERFECT SCENARIO, A TEA HOUSE (SEE PAGES 148–57). FOR MOST PEOPLE, HOWEVER, THE VIEW IS OF THE BUILDING NEXT DOOR OR THE NEIGHBOR'S FENCE OR A PARKED CAR WITH JUST A HINT OF A TREE TOP IN THE DISTANCE.

TO CREATE THE ILLUSION OF A NATURAL ENVIRONMENT AND PEACEFUL, LIGHT, SERENE SURROUNDINGS THERE ARE A NUMBER OF OPTICAL AND DECORATING TRICKS THAT CAN BE EMPLOYED AND THESE ARE DESCRIBED IN THIS CHAPTER. THERE ARE ALSO WAYS OF INCREASING THE LIGHT THAT IS AVAILABLE, NOT JUST BY ADDING OR OPENING UP WINDOWS, BUT WITH THE SKILLFUL USE OF MIRRORS AND REFLECTIVE SURFACES.

IF YOUR WINDOWS LOOK OUT ONTO A BLANK WALL, FIND OUT IF IT IS POSSIBLE TO PAINT IT WHITE OR A PALE COLOR SO THAT IT REFLECTS LIGHT BACK INTO YOUR ROOM. IF PAINTING IS NOT AN OPTION, APPROACH YOUR NEIGHBOR OR LANDLORD ABOUT GROWING A VINE OR CREEPING PLANT UP THE WALL SO THAT THE OUTLOOK IS MORE INTERESTING AND WILL HAVE SEASONAL VARIATIONS AS LEAVES TURN TO FALL COLORS OR FLOWERS BLOOM. BEWARE OF SOME IVIES AND CLIMBING PLANTS BECAUSE THEY CAN TAKE HOLD IN THE GAPS BETWEEN THE BRICKS AND CAUSE STRUCTURAL DAMAGE.

The flow of natural light through this building creates shadows and reflections that play along the plain walls and polished floors. The use of reinforced glass panelling at the edge of the staircase and on the upper level enhances the feeling of space and echoes the water in the pool beneath.

& ILLUSION

RIGHT: When the climate is fine these glass-panelled doors can be folded back so that the room becomes part of the outdoors. When the weather is too cold to have them open, the glass doors still allow the bather the view and the impression of being in the garden.

RIGHT: In this traditional Zen-style room the panels can also be slid to the side making the room and the outside into one space. To further enhance this, the flooring both inside and out are on the same level and made of the same material.

If these two options don't have any result, set about creating the illusion from inside your own home. If the view is industrial or depressing, try screening the window with a large sheet (or a patchwork of several smaller pieces) of opaque white paper. There are many attractive handmade papers that have strands of silk or dried flower petals incorporated within their structure. With this sort of screen you are not losing space because the paper can be fixed directly to the window frame, and because the paper is light, daylight will still pass through. The texture or finish of the paper will be highlighted by the light and the whole piece will appear framed, like a picture, by the woodwork on the outer edges of the window.

If the view is bearable but unappealing, and the maximum amount of daylight is necessary, fix two or three rows of shelves across the window, leaving space between to allow access to the catches should you need to open the window. Ideally, the shelves should be made of reinforced glass so that light is not hindered and they appear almost invisible to the eye. On these shelves you can then display glass—clear, colored, or a mix of vases, bottles, drinking glasses or lightweight, transparent *objets d'art*. The light will pass through the glass objects but they will form a screen or closer level of focus so that the outside world becomes secondary. If the glass objects fill the shelf space adequately they will also give a certain amount of privacy from the gazes of passers-by.

If you have a tree top view or a pleasant aspect of scudding clouds in the sky, but the lower half of the vista is filled with construction, roof tops, or rows of parked cars, concentrate your focus on the pleasant aspects by putting a small half-curtain, or appropriate size of hanging, over the lower part of the window. The eye will then automatically go to the upper part and the pleasant view.

Plants can also be arranged on shelves constructed across a window, or use them on their own to form a natural screen of greenery and leaves. Wide, frondy ferns are generally perfect for this sort of job, although too much direct sunlight can be detrimental as they are shade-loving plants.

For a more permanent green display and barrier, plant window boxes with dwarf shrubs and miniature trees, or fill them with a

seasonal selection of flowers and bulbs so that you have a different outlook at various times of the year. The boxes can also be planted with seeds and cuttings appropriate to the room that they are outside. For example, put herbs in a box or pots outside the kitchen window, and for the summer evenings, plant scented flowers such as night-scented stock outside a bedroom window so that the delicate, floral scent will waft in through the window on the warm evening air.

Glass bricks are another useful way of obscuring an unpleasant view but nevertheless allowing in light. The thick, opaque bricks can be clear or tinted with a pale wash of color and are ideal to inset into a pavement above a basement apartment or in a wall where security, as well as light, is important. Set the glass bricks into a surround of red bricks or breeze blocks so that there are no openings or catches to be forced by would-be-burglars. Safety-wise, glass bricks are so thick, they are very difficult to break.

Also use glass bricks to create a shower wall in a bathroom or a divide or surround in a kitchen. They are especially effective in the bathroom because of their water-like appearance. Again, light will be able to pass through them from a window to the far side of the room and because they are thick they offer a certain amount of privacy. They are also resistant to the effects of regular water use and can be easily cleaned.

USING REFLECTIVE SURFACES

Mirrors have long had magical associations, from fairy tales to wizardry, and used in the right way they, too, create illusions of space and light. For example, a good-sized mirror positioned on the wall opposite a window reflects the light, doubling its effect. The mirror will also give the appearance of a second window, creating a "view" from the reflection.

This use of mirror is ideal for a long narrow passageway or corridor. By placing a large mirror at the end of the hallway to maximize the amount of reflective surface, the light from any source is amplified, whether through an open door, a window opposite, or a central electric light. Use pale or white paintwork to enhance the illusion of light, and the mirror will further create the impression that the hall is longer than it really is, disappearing into the distance. An illusion of space is also achieved by placing two mirrors opposite each other to produce a never-ending image reflected in itself over and over again.

To compose an interesting and unusual effect with mirrors, group together a number of smaller mirrors on a wall and the reflection is multiplied so there are several reflections instead of just one. This can be especially effective if the mirrors are arranged so that they have a specific focus, such as of a beautiful painting, photograph, or flower suitably positioned opposite or in front of the mirror.

Another useful reflective surface is stainless steel, now popular in kitchen design. Although some finishes soften the brilliance of a highly polished reflective surface, the inherent qualities of the steel will cause a certain amount of light to "bounce" back, even if the sheen has been dulled. Silver, copper, and brass also reflect light as, to a lesser extent, do polished marble, enamel, or other glazed surfaces. Dull finishes such as concrete or roughly finished plaster and dark colors absorb light, which can make them appear dense and oddly velvety or soft to the touch.

This glass brick inner wall blocks the view but allows light to pass through which is ideal in a narrow galley kitchen-cum-dining space or a kitchen area at the end of a corridor. The neat uniform surfaces of the units also help reflect light and promote the impression of space.

THE BENEFITS OF COLOR

The use of color is another practical way of making a room appear to have proportions different from those actually present. By painting a high ceiling in a rich, dark tone, it can be softened and optically lowered. To make the walls feel shorter, apply the same dark color on the lower half of the wall beneath the dado level. Use lighting, too, to further these effects (see pages 60–7).

In a small room, keep colors light to create a feeling of space. A white ceiling will appear further away; painting a band around the top of the ceiling in white will also add to the illusion of height. Conversely, make a long room feel shorter by painting a strong, bright color on the far wall, which makes it seem to be closer. Use floorboards to further these effects. If the planks are laid in vertical lines parallel to the longest wall of a room they make the place seem longer. Conversely, if they are placed horizontally across the point of entrance they make the room seem wider.

The illusion of a certain type of atmosphere or environment is also created through color. Particular shades of blue can feel cold to some people, others may find it restful, reminiscent of water and its gentle flow. Orange can make you feel hot, agitated and over-stimulated, yet others feel it emits a cozy and comforting aura. Dark red often gets a similar response; it can be enveloping, contemplative, and reassuring or at the other extreme, claustrophobic. So when choosing a strong or dominant color for a room, make sure it is one that you and your family feel comfortable with. Ask others for their response to the color before applying it to the walls.

METHOD

ZEN IS ABOUT FREEING-UP THE MIND AND THE SPIRIT, WHICH IN TURN MEANS MAKING YOUR SURROUNDINGS LESS COMPLEX AND DEMANDING. THE ZEN PHILOSOPHY IS THAT PEOPLE CAN BECOME TOO WEIGHED DOWN BY POSSESSIONS, SO WHERE POSSIBLE THEY SHOULD BE EDITED AND ELIMINATED. THIS DOES NOT HAVE TO MEAN A FRUGAL OR COMFORTLESS HOME, BUT BY STORING AND CONCEALING ITEMS YOU CAN GIVE AN IMPRESSION OF SPACE, LIGHT, AND OPENNESS. YOU ALSO CREATE A GREATER SENSE OF ORDER, WHICH IS PEACEFUL IN ITS OWN RIGHT.

THE TWENTIETH-CENTURY HOME IS A PLACE FULL OF THE PARAPHERNALIA OF LIFE, RANGING FROM BOOKS, CDS, CLOTHES, DECORATIVE OBJECTS, VIDEO TAPES, AND MAGAZINES TO PILLS, POTIONS, SHAMPOOS, CREAMS, AND NUMEROUS OTHER ITEMS OF KITCHEN AND ELECTRONIC EQUIPMENT. TO KEEP THESE IN ORDER AND ULTIMATELY TO MAKE THEM MORE ACCESSIBLE, GOOD STORAGE IS ESSENTIAL, BUT THIS ALWAYS HAS TO BE PLANNED FOR.

THE SIMPLEST WAY TO DO THIS IS TO TAKE EACH ROOM IN TURN. PUT THE CONTENTS OF EXISTING CABINETS AND SHELVES INTO A CENTRAL PILE, THEN LOOK AT EACH ITEM IN TURN AND ASK YOURSELF THESE QUESTIONS: WHEN DID I LAST USE/WEAR THIS? WILL I NEED IT AGAIN IN THE FUTURE? WHY HAVE I KEPT IT? DOES IT REALLY BELONG IN THIS ROOM? IF YOU STILL FEEL YOU NEED TO KEEP THE ITEM, PUT IT TO ONE SIDE. ONCE THE EDIT IS COMPLETE, GET RID OF EVERYTHING. TAKE THE OBJECTS THAT AREN'T NEEDED TO A LOCAL CHARITY SHOP OR TAG SALE. WHATEVER ELSE YOU DO, DON'T KEEP THEM IN BOXES IN THE GARAGE JUST IN CASE YOU SHOULD EVER NEED THEM AGAIN!

Storage does not need to be dull. Deep drawers like these can be arranged to form an interesting feature on a wall, as well as being useful for containing smaller items of clothing such as socks, T-shirts, underwear, and shirts.

& ORDER

If jars of dried goods and ingredients are to be left on show they will appear neat and less obtrusive if they are stored in similar containers. Here, matching rows of glass jars look pleasing but also allow the person preparing food to know, at a glance, exactly which ingredient is where.

Putting items where they belong, in terms of use, is often beneficial, not least because they will then be always close to hand when you need them. By categorizing things into work, rest, and play sections you can, more or less, house them in separate compartments. Of course, some things cross over, but if the bulk stays together, some form of order has been achieved. As the saying goes, "a place for everything and everything in its place".

KITCHEN STORAGE

In the kitchen, the division of items can be difficult. It is best to keep utensils in areas where they are used. For example, store tongs, oven mitts, spatulas, and cooking tools by the oven and stove; table cutlery and china near the table, and food storage near the fridge so that when you unpack the week's shopping you can unload it all in one area instead of having to dash backwards and forwards across the room.

Deep drawers often invite chaos because they tempt clutter to accumulate. If the drawer is subdivided or filled with smaller boxes or mini-crates, each section can be allocated a specific purpose, such as pens and pencils or knives, forks and spoons. Next time you open the drawer thinking you'll have to search for something, you will be pleasantly surprised to find whatever it is you want, instantly and clearly visible.

Shelves create the same problem as they tempt you to stuff things into them rather than storing them in an orderly fashion. Like the drawers, sub-divide them. Keep magazines in stacking boxes and papers in files. For kitchen cupboards, fix a covered metal hanging shelf below an upper shelf giving you a two-shelf capacity in one. If the shelves are very widely spaced you may choose to put in a permanent mid-way shelf.

Only keep items that are used and washed regularly on display or on open shelves. The kitchen is a place where grease and dust quickly accumulate and things that stay in one place for long easily become covered in a film of sticky sediment.

Certain items of dried food can be stored in an attractive way that will make them an integral part of the decor of the room. Orange and black lentils, flageolet and butter beans, red kidney beans and dried pasta can all look interesting both in color and texture. To create a feeling of uniformity, which in itself gives an impression of order, ensure your storage containers are identical or as similar as possible, whether you opt for simple glass jars or stainless steel canisters.

BEDROOM STORAGE

In the case of a bedroom, the divisions are best made into types of clothing, accessories, and shoes. Assess the storage you have, and ask yourself if it is well positioned and practical. Hanging space may best be halved so that you can keep one vertical section for full-length coats and dresses but have two shorter horizontal hanging sections, one above the other, for shirts, skirts and folded trousers. To help keep the contents of drawers organized, use specifically designed dividers, just as for the kitchen.

Hanging shoe shelves are also a practical way of keeping pairs together and at hand, rather than getting down on your hands and knees to rummage in the back of a dark, dusty closet for the missing half. These long canvas panels are sectioned into pockets, each big

RIGHT: By keeping the drawer faces and cabinet doors in the same clean and understated finish this wall of storage becomes almost invisible.

RIGHT ABOVE: When the lid of the vanity unit is closed, it provides a clean surface on which to stack towels or clothes.

BELOW: The lid is lifted and the double basins are revealed and ready for use.

enough for a pair of shoes. They can be hung from a rail inside the wardrobe or behind a bedroom or dressing room door.

Where possible, try to keep as many of your possessions as you can in cabinets or behind doors to keep dust from accumulating and to give the impression of as large an amount of room as possible. Fitted wardrobes and cabinets can take up space and make an already small room feel even smaller. To counteract this, cover the door panels with mirrors, which will not only be useful to check your appearance but also to reflect light from the windows and the image of the room, making the place seem lighter and larger.

Under-bed storage is another good hiding place. Some beds already have drawers fitted into the base or you can buy flat, high-sided wooden boxes on rollers or opaque plastic boxes with lids that come on castors, so they are easily retrieved from under the bed for use or when cleaning.

GENERAL STORAGE IDEAS

In most modern or minimalist homes there are walls of panels, which at first glance appear to be part of the structure of the place yet, at a finger's touch, the panels open to reveal ample storage space. This is the secret of how these minimalist homes always look so devoid of clutter. Creating concealed storage like this is difficult in a small apartment where the rooms may not be deep enough to cope with such built-in cabinets or in an old building where the walls are uneven or interrupted by features such as chimneys. But by using panels of roller blinds or tab-top cotton curtains you could achieve a similar, but softer, storage system.

There are certain possessions that have a seasonal life, such as heavy quilts, overcoats, wool scarves, hammocks, and cotton summer dresses. Fold these away carefully and neatly into dust covers or lidded boxes to keep them tidy and clean. Then store them in places that are perhaps less easily or regularly accessible—the sort of place where you probably have to get a chair or ladder to reach. There is often under-utilized storage in the uppermost reaches of a closet or built-in wardrobe, but because you only have to have access to them once or twice a year the extra effort required to get them up and down is minimal.

The long bench in front of the book case could be used for three different functions. First it could be used as a seat if you wish to read a book from the shelf; it may also double as a desk, as a place to layout paperwork or notes, and if the lid is lifted the base could also be used for storage.

The peg rail, a simple storage idea used extensively by the Shakers, can be used for practically anything and almost anywhere. In Shaker homes, lightweight rail-back chairs were hung on the pegs so that the floor could be easily and effectively cleaned. Use peg rails anywhere from the bathroom, where damp towels can be stretched across two or three pegs to air and dry, to the hallway where often-used coats and jackets need to be at hand.

CREATING ORDER THROUGH DISPLAY

There is an art to displaying items, as described on pages 138–47, and in the simple and uncluttered surroundings of the Zen home the few, simple objects that you choose to display become important because the setting and background offers little distraction to the eye. You will find that odd numbers of items, usually threes or fives, make a more pleasing group than even numbers.

The creative arrangement of objects introduces a note of serenity to a room. Straightforward, everyday items such as glasses, flowers, fruit, or shells often make the most effective still lifes. The impact is in the way they are grouped or arranged and the blending of harmonious colors and shapes that will relate to one another and to the space around them.

A combined storage and display area is another way of cutting down on clutter because the two requirements are fulfilled by a single piece of furniture. The typical Asian answer to this quandary is a simple oblong chest. It can be made of many materials such as plain, lacquered, painted, or fabric-covered wood or more lightweight materials such as bamboo or wicker. Use the inside of the chest to keep a selection of small, special items and the lid, when closed, becomes the area on which some or all are displayed as the mood takes you. The old-fashioned blanket chest is a similarly useful object, as the box can be used to store heavy winter blankets or quilts when not in use, but placed at the foot of the bed it doubles as a seat or a place to lay out clothes.

Once you have started to organize and edit your possessions you will probably find that you actually need less storage space because you have fewer items. And those that you do have, are neatly and economically stored.

Z

E

N

SPACE

IN ZEN TERMS, THE EFFICIENT USE OF SPACE AND AIR IS BENEFICIAL FOR THE GENERAL WELL-BEING OF A PERSON, BOTH MENTALLY AND PHYSICALLY, AND FOR THE ENERGIES OR LIFE FORCES KNOWN AS CHI (PRONOUNCED AS *CHEE*). CHI FLOWS EVERYWHERE AND WHERE IT MEETS OR CONCENTRATES, THINGS FLOURISH. FLOWING WATER IS A STRONG CHI FORCE, AS IS MOVING OR CIRCULATING AIR. STAGNANT WATER AND AIR DO NOT PROMOTE GROWTH OR STIMULATION. INSTEAD, THE CHI LOOSES ITS RESILIENCE AND DECAYS, WHICH CREATES AN AREA WHERE PLANTS DIE, OUR MOODS MAY BECOME DOWNCAST AND OUR ABILITY TO GROW OR ADVANCE IS ARRESTED.

FOR A PHYSICAL FEELING OF WELL-BEING, AN INCREASED MOVEMENT OF AIR HELPS THE EVAPORATION OF MOISTURE FROM THE SKIN AND BRINGS OXYGENATED AIR INTO THE LUNGS, WHICH MAKES YOU FEEL INVIGORATED AND ALERT. TO PROMOTE THIS HEALTHY ENVIRONMENT, IT IS IMPORTANT TO TRY TO ACHIEVE AN EFFICIENT SYSTEM OF AIR FLOW AND CROSS-VENTILATION.

IN EARLIER TIMES, THERE WAS PLENTY OF VENTILATION THROUGH HOMES, MOSTLY BECAUSE THEY WERE BUILT OF NATURAL, BREATHABLE MATERIALS SUCH AS WOOD, STRAW AND CLAY, AND THE BUILDINGS WERE DRAFTY AND SELDOM AIR-TIGHT. IN MODERN TIMES, WINDOWS ARE DOUBLE-GLAZED AND SEALED, DOORS FIT TIGHT SHUT, AND INSULATION IS PUT OVER AND UNDER THE BREATHABLE MATERIALS OF BRICK WALLS AND SLATE ROOFING TILES TO KEEP THE COLD OUT AND THE HEAT IN. THE BUILD-UP OF STALE AIR AND NOXIOUS GASES ACCUMULATES QUICKLY AND CAN BE DETRIMENTAL TO A PERSON'S HEALTH, SO A CONSTANT FLOW OF AIR IS NECESSARY, ESPECIALLY IN MODERN HOMES.

The main floor area of this room is left free of furniture or clutter. The simple screen, low table, and cushions are placed on a raised dais at the end of the room and may be closed off behind the sliding screens.

& FLOW

Good air flow through open internal doors helps heating to circulate and has the added benefit of keeping the temperature constant, rather than variable, from room to room. The flow of cooler air into a room causes heated air to rise, which in turn is pushed out by warmer air that rises to replace it, so setting up a circular movement. Sitting in a poorly ventilated, over-heated room makes you drowsy and dehydrated; it is often better to put on a jumper or do some exercise than turn the heating too high.

In rooms where there are electrically powered machines such as a television, computer, or microwave, good ventilation is of particular importance because the area around the machine has an electric field, which can be positively or negatively charged. When particles become charged in the field they are ionized and create the phenomenon known as static electricity. This can cause shocks to be given when the skin comes in to contact with plastic, synthetic fibers, foam-backed rugs or carpets, and certain metals.

Static electricity builds up over time in a poorly ventilated room, but will be discharged by water or other similar conductors. So taking a bath or shower (fast flowing water is also an initiator of good Chi) or walking around barefoot on a natural floor covering such as wooden floorboards or sisal matting (synthetic carpet will only encourage the static) negates the charge. Ionizers, small devices that can be easily installed in any room, also help to keep static at bay by putting negative ions into the air.

The furniture in this room has been arranged to create two small sitting rooms within the main space. It has also been positioned so that there is plenty of space and air between each piece, which creates a feeling of airiness and light.

Where gas heaters, stoves, central heating and boilers are in use, it is vital that a through-flow of air is available because burning gas can emit toxic fumes such as carbon monoxide, carbon dioxide, and nitric oxide. Buy all appliances with approved safety warrants and have them regularly checked; at the first detection of any unexpected smell of gas call the local gas authority.

To prevent the accumulation of moisture that can lead to condensation and the growth of mold, efficient ventilation is particularly necessary in bathrooms and kitchens. The passing air will also help disperse any cooking smells or odors as well as the build-up of heat, which can become overpowering if a number of stove rings and an oven are all on at the same time in a small room.

Ventilation can be aided by electric fans and air conditioning units but it is cheaper and more environmentally friendly to try and accomplish it by opening windows and doors. For security you may need to install shutters or lattice work screens over windows on lower floors. In areas where the heat can be intense, these window treatments also provide cool and shade.

Although doors need to be closed at certain times to give privacy or quiet, they should be left open as much as possible. Similarly, if windows cannot be left wholly open, then they are best left ajar or at least opened at the upper level so that air can flow through. In an ideal scenario, windows are best left open at opposite sides of the house with an uninterrupted passageway between.

Use a fan to further aid the movement of air, turning it on as and when it is needed. Central ceiling fans can be decorative and useful in tropical climates. But for more seasonal use, floor standing fans with a revolving head provide an effective local air stir, and desk-top fans are efficient, especially during the summer.

ARRANGING FURNITURE BENEFICIALLY

The overall organization of rooms in your home will benefit the through-flow of air, and can add to the feeling of well-being and light. When you open a door and enter a room there should be a clear space in front of you, not the back of an armchair or a table, which will inhibit or bar your entrance. It is also unsettling for someone sitting in front of the door not to be able to see who is entering.

By placing the two armchairs along the wall opposite the two-seater sofa there is a feeling of balance. The central floor area has also been left relatively clear so that on entering the room there is an impression of space and light.

If the dynamics of the room prevents a clear entrance, create a screen that will "protect" the back of the person sitting but act as a welcoming sight to the person who is arriving. This can be done by placing a table behind the chair and arranging on it a diaphanous fern or a group of tall vases. A mirror on the wall opposite the door and chair will also help counteract the feeling of being blocked or hemmed in around the doorway. Even if the entrance is clear, the eyes of the person entering the room should be drawn to something inviting such as a flickering fire in a hearth, an attractive piece of pottery, or a scented bloom, which is pleasurable and encouraging.

Position low furniture around a window so that the light and air coming through are not blocked or hindered. Built-in window seats are ideal as not only can storage space be built underneath but they fit in neatly beneath the sill and offer a perfect perch from which to enjoy a view and sunlight.

Try to arrange your furniture so that it presents an overall impression of being balanced. Don't cram all the chairs and sofas in front of the fire or in one corner. Instead, spread them out so that

LEFT: A set of narrow shelves acts as a room divider between areas with different functions yet it does not block out the light or cut one area off from the other. Some shelves are left empty and others are simply decorated with low items at around eye level and taller items above, so that visual contact can be maintained with people in both halves of the room.

LEFT: These archways help give definition to the spaces between them. In the foreground, the pillar creates a barrier between the dining table and the hallway and the four pillars behind define the boundary of the sitting room.

there is air and space between each piece. Clutter is a stagnant feature in a room and consequently creates poor Chi energy, which can lead to negative or depressed feelings.

Ideally, keep a passageway clear from one side of the room to the other so that it is easy to cross the space without having to tackle an obstacle course of stepping over a low stool or table, and swerving around sofas and chairs.

A clear passageway can also make a small room seem larger as it draws the eye to a length of line or space. Avoid clutter on the floor and don't leave stacks of newspapers or small decorative objects around as they can be damaged by an accidental kick or cause someone to fall.

CREATING A SPACE WITHIN A SPACE

In a one-room apartment or within a large room in a house you may like to create inner sanctums. Use the whole room when you are entertaining but you may find that a smaller and cozier inner space can

be more relaxing when alone or with a friend. Create the inner room by reducing the gap that lies between two sofas and bringing them face to face or removing the barrier of a coffee table or similar piece. You could also move two chairs into a corner so that the walls form a protective backdrop behind the occupants.

Alternatively, create a room within a room with sliding screens or panels. Lightweight portable screens are very useful because they can be folded up and stacked away flat when they are not needed. Mobile bookcases, mounted on four sturdy wheels—or castors that have locks so that they can be secured when in place—are another handy way of creating a more intimate space when it is required.

Further define these areas by using mats or rugs. For example, if you have a wooden floor throughout, define the dining area by placing the table and chairs on a rug of one color. Treat the sitting area in the same way, with the furniture arranged around another mat of a similar or contrasting color. In this way, the uncovered wooden floor that lies between the two spaces becomes an empty, free-flowing pathway.

LIGHT

Light can also mean heat and in the height of summer it may be necessary to restrict the flow of light in to a room in order to maintain a comfortable room temperature.

LIGHT IS A VITAL INGREDIENT IN DAILY LIFE AND OUR PRIMARY SOURCE OF ILLUMINATION AS WELL AS A GIVER OF HEAT. LIGHT STIMULATES THE SENSE OF SIGHT, ENCOURAGES PLANTS AND OTHER LIVING THINGS TO GROW, AND ALONG WITH WATER AND AIR IT IS AN ESSENTIAL ELEMENT IN MAINTAINING HEALTH AND VITALITY. MOST LIVING ORGANISMS NEED LIGHT TO FUNCTION. PLANTS, PEOPLE, AND ANIMALS RESPOND POSITIVELY TO DAYLIGHT NOT ONLY IN TERMS OF GROWTH BUT ALSO IN LESS OBVIOUS WAYS, SUCH AS THE ACTIVITIES OF DIGESTION AND HORMONE EFFICIENCY. AS SUCH, IT IS AN ESSENTIAL ELEMENT OF THE ZEN INTERIOR.

SUNLIGHT IS ALSO FREE, SO IT IS ECONOMICAL TO MAKE THE BEST AND MOST EFFICIENT USE OF IT THAT YOU CAN. LIGHT, WHETHER NATURAL OR MAN-MADE, IS EMITTED FROM A SOURCE IN STRAIGHT LINES AND SPREADS OUT OVER AN INCREASINGLY LARGE AREA AS IT TRAVELS. WHEN LIGHT COMES IN CONTACT WITH A SURFACE IT IS EITHER ABSORBED OR REFLECTED AND SO TEXTURES AND FINISHES WILL EFFECT THE WAY LIGHT RESPONDS. A SMOOTH SHINY SURFACE, FOR EXAMPLE, PROVIDES A CERTAIN AMOUNT OF REFLECTION, WHEREAS A ROUGH OR TEXTURED SURFACE CAUSES MORE OF THE LIGHT TO BE ABSORBED. COLORS HAVE THE SAME EFFECT: LIGHT COLORS WILL REFLECT, AND DARK COLORS, ESPECIALLY BLACK, ABSORB.

DAYLIGHT IS ALSO A CONSTANTLY CHANGING SOURCE OF ILLUMINATION— CHANGING IN DIRECTION, INTENSITY, AND THE WAY IT EFFECTS COLORS. FROM THE GLARING BRIGHT LIGHT OF A SUNNY MIDDAY IN SUMMER, IT ALTERS TO PINKISH AND GOLDEN HUES AT SUNSET.

& NATURAL

RIGHT: Keeping clutter away from the area immediately in front of the window allows the maximum amount of daylight into the room. Although it is invigorating to wake up in sunlight, the window may need to be screened for privacy. Use adjustable blinds or opaque glass in the lower frames.

FAR RIGHT: Roller blinds take up little space but are easily adjusted or rolled back out of the way as and when they are needed.

The changing light also creates varying areas and depth of shape; part of a room may appear light in the spring but be dull and dark in the winter. In many ways, these seasonal changes reflect the natural cycle of life. In the shorter winter days, the feeling of hibernation, introspection and hominess is predominant, whereas in the spring and summer the feeling is of vitality and outdoor activities.

Lack of daylight is linked with Seasonal Affective Disorder, known as SAD, which is most common in winter and characterized by depressions, increased sleepiness, fatigue, and weight gain. Treatment for sufferers includes sitting in front of a bright full-spectrum light for at least two hours a day. Even if you don't suffer from this severe form of light deprivation you can take steps to make your home light and energizing so that the gray, winter days will be less gloomy.

ENHANCING NATURAL LIGHT

Take a long look at your rooms and think how they are used. If you have a desk or favorite chair for reading, it is best placed by a window instead of deeper in the room where light may be cut off by a high chair back, bookcase, or other tall piece of furniture. Also, if the chair is at the far side of the room from the window, the light will have further to travel and its power will be reduced.

Make sure your windows are free of clutter, both inside and out. Hold back curtains and hangings to the outer edge of the frames and remove valances that cover the upper parts of windows. Also check vegetation outside: trees, hedges, and vines can block out light as they grow.

Reflective surfaces such as mirrors are a simple but effective way of doubling the amount of available light (see pages 60–7). Likewise, light colors are effective reflectors, which is why white gloss paint is most commonly found around a window frame and sill. Although net or voile curtains may be needed for privacy, try hanging a half curtain rather than filling the whole window. Most obviously, but still worth mentioning, keep the windows themselves sparkling clean. Rain and traffic pollution soon build up a fine film on the outside of the glass and wood fires or grease from cooking can affect the inside.

Pools of artificial light, from recessed down lighters, are used to accent and highlight areas of this room as well as ensuring that the steps are clearly visible and safe to use.

There are many types of artificial light and some are best suited to specific tasks. The three main types are background, task, and mood. Background lighting is used to cover a large area, in effect to give general light to a whole room. The most common form of this lighting is a central fitting that hangs from the ceiling. But this can produce an unsubtle and bland spread of light that is acceptable only as a temporary form of illumination.

Create a more subtle and atmospheric style by using a combination of uplighters, table, and wall lights, which can give a similar overall strength of light but at a variety of levels. Wire the lights onto circuits that are operated from a single switch panel so that you don't have to turn on each light individually. By adding a dimmer switch to the circuit you can also vary the intensity of the light to suit your mood.

Task lighting is a concentrated light source such as a spotlight or reading light. This type of light is essential in a kitchen to cast a bright, non-shadow forming beam on to the work top and stove to prevent accidents when using sharp knives and boiling liquids. Also in this category are picture lights, which can be targeted on paintings, pictures, or decorative objects. Tiny, low-voltage halogen lights as well as the more traditional spotlights are both suited to this job.

Mood lighting is important in Zen interiors because it creates an ambience or setting. Most lights can be used with a dimmer switch to give a variety of moods. For example, table lamps, at eye level when sitting, will create immediate pools of light, leaving the upper regions of the room and areas furthest away from the light source in shadow, which can make an intimate and cozy atmosphere. Candlelight is another source of mood lighting that can also be calming, but carefully position them so as not to be a fire hazard.

Choosing the right bulb is also essential for achieving the appropriate strength and balance of light. Low-voltage halogen bulbs produce a bright, white light suitable for task lighting. Halogen also gives a bright white light and is best suited to uplighters. Tungsten is the most common light bulb and gives a warm, yellowish light. Fluorescent lights vary in color but tend to be used most commonly in strip lights, which are useful in under unit lighting in a kitchen but can look unsightly if they are used in the center of a ceiling. There are also daylight or full-spectrum light bulbs, which emulate natural light and can be beneficial to sufferers of SAD.

Overhead skylights or a glazed atrium give a regular and constant source of daylight. Where light comes in through windows at the sides of a house the brightness will be less predictable as it will move and decline as the sun moves away from that side of the building. As with a flow of air, however, leaving internal doors open can help light travel from one area to another.

When it comes to the fabric and furnishing of a room, plan it to encourage and increase the flow and amount of natural light. Light colors and a proportion of reflective rather than absorbent fabrics will help.

USING ELECTRIC LIGHTS

Once you have studied how to make the best use of natural light within your room, turn your attention to the positioning and use of artificial or electric lights. Use them to create a theater of light with highlights, focal points, shafts of light, and dramatic contrasts, as well as a subtle, relaxing, and calming ambient, background illumination.

For example, although the damp and warmth of the bathroom can be beneficial to ferns and orchids, this particular environment is not too good for cacti, which like to grow in a dry atmosphere. Some plants prefer shade to light and others a cooler rather than warm environment. If you are putting plants on a windowsill, make sure they are sun loving and that you rotate and water them regularly. Avoid putting plants or vases of flowers on electrical equipment such as the television or over a shelf of hi-fi equipment as any drops of water splashing around during watering may damage the equipment, and heat and radiation emitted when the machines are in use could adversely affect the plant.

Indoor plants are also beneficial to the environment and atmosphere of the rooms where they stand because they filter and purify the air. Through photosynthesis, plants convert sunlight into chemical energy and in the process they absorb carbon monoxide in the air, replacing it with oxygen. Plants can also add to the humidity of a room, not only through the water that you put on them but also through their leaves.

NATURE'S WAY

Houseplants bring living color into the home. Watching the colors change with the seasons, or gradually revealing a flower from a bud is therapeutic and keeps you in touch with the cycle of nature. To grow plants successfully indoors you should match the type of plant to the environment in which it is to be placed.

PART TWO
APPLICATION

WAY IN

THE WAY INTO YOUR HOME IS NOT ONLY THE FIRST IMPRESSION A VISITOR RECEIVES ABOUT YOU AND YOUR PERSONAL SPACE BUT IT IS ALSO THE THING THAT GREETS YOU EACH TIME YOU RETURN HOME, SO IT SHOULD BE WELCOMING, INVITING, AND RELAXING. THE INITIAL IMPACT IS IMPORTANT AS IT SETS THE TONE AND SUMS UP THE STYLE OF THE REST OF THE DWELLING. TO BRING THE ZEN PRINCIPLES INTO PLAY IN THE EXTERIOR AREA, SOME LIVING ELEMENT WOULD BE APPROPRIATE SUCH AS A SMALL WILLOW TREE, A WOODEN CONTAINER PLANTED WITH A GROUP OF SINGLE COLORED BULBS, A POND OR WATER FEATURE, OR A PATH OF ROUNDED PEBBLES.

THE FRONT DOOR IS THE FIRST BARRIER AND AS SUCH IT SHOULD BE PRACTICAL AND STURDY, BUT NOT INTIMIDATING. SO AN AUSPICIOUS AND HOSPITABLE COLOR OR PROTECTIVELY SEALED NATURAL WOODEN DOOR WITH A BRIGHT DECORATION SUCH AS A SHINING BRASS OR CHROME HANDLE OR LETTERBOX WILL GIVE IT A CRISP AND CLEAN BUT PLEASANT GREETING.

A hallway is the first point of entry for both you and your guests. It should be warm and welcoming but not cluttered or difficult to move through. It should also be light and easy to come to terms with, within moments of arriving.

THE FRONT DOOR MAY OPEN INTO A HALLWAY OR DIRECTLY INTO A ROOM, DEPENDING ON THE STYLE OF THE BUILDING. A HALLWAY IS A BUFFER BETWEEN THE OUTER AND INNER WORLDS AND MAY BE THE PLACE WHERE YOU TAKE OFF COATS, JACKETS, BOOTS, AND SHOES, SO STORAGE IS AN IMPORTANT CONSIDERATION. TO KEEP TO THE ZEN IDEALS OF SPACIOUSNESS AND LACK OF CLUTTER, CONCEAL COATS AND SHOES IN A CLOSET RATHER THAN HUNG ON NUMEROUS PEGS OR LEFT DRAPED OVER FURNITURE IN THE HALLWAY. PILING UP LAYERS OF THICK COATS IN A NARROW HALLWAY ALSO CUTS DOWN ON THE THROUGH-FLOW OF LIGHT AND PEOPLE BECAUSE IT REDUCES THE AMOUNT OF SPACE AND PRESENTS OBSTACLES.

In a wide hallway it may be possible to annex off a small area to make a walk-in closet. This will not only keep the clothes and shoes out of the way but will create a feature in an otherwise open but under-utilized space. By using opaque Plexiglas or reinforced glass to make the walls of the cloakroom, the light from the hall can be used as additional illumination in the cloakroom and make the place seem less dense. If the area around the door is roomy enough, then a small shelf for keys and mail can be useful but it should not become a dumping ground. A single chair or stool, a place of repose after the journey home, is a symbolic gesture of welcome as well as a useful place to sit when putting on shoes and boots.

Try to keep furniture in the hallway to a minimum so that there is an appearance of space and openness. The hall and entrance are not designed to be places for gatherings or long periods of sitting so avoid encouraging these things by keeping seats, tables, and other places where you can lean or rest to a minimum. Instead, the hallway and corridor is where most traffic passes through—people, children, dogs, and visitors, all coming and going. If there are obstructions such as unwieldy pieces of furniture that jut out into the hallway or rows of shoes in a random stack by the door, these will add to the physical and mental stress of leaving and arriving.

If the front door opens directly into a room, try to create a place of welcome and introduction immediately inside the door. This can be done by placing a mat, preferably a round one, at the threshold. A mat forms a symbolic point of entry or departure and if it is round suggests a full stop, or place to slow down. Make sure that any mats or runners by the door are securely fixed, especially if placed on a varnished or polished wood floor. There are a number of double-sided carpet tapes as well as non-slip backings that can be put on the reverse side of floor coverings. While on the subject of safety, if there are steps leading up to the front door on the outside or down from the door on the inside, keep them well-lit to avoid stumbling or tripping.

CHOOSING FLOORING

A long hallway offers the promise of a journey, so use a runner or length of mat to emphasize the feeling of a path leading away from the door and into the inner and more intimate parts of the house.

By replacing the solid sides of a staircase with a banister and high tension wire, light is allowed to travel freely from the front of the hallway through to the back. The stairs become an integral part of the hallway rather than a dark, boxed-off passageway.

Symbolically, the mat can also represent a bridge from the outside to the inner sanctum.

If the hallway is long, clutter-free, and with high ceilings, it may be noisy, with sound echoing off the hard surfaces. A mat or runner will also help to dampen the sound and make foot steps muffled and less obvious. In pure Zen interiors, the matting is tatami made from woven rushes, which has a warm, soft, and slightly springy quality underfoot. Because tatami matting is light it can also be easily removed to be shaken and cleaned outdoors.

A polished or sealed wood floor is the ideal for a Zen-inspired hallway. Not only does it introduce the element of nature, it also offers color and pattern. The way the boards or planks of wood are arranged can create a subtle but interesting design. For example, if the planks are laid lengthwise along the hall they make it appear longer and if laid widthwise, a narrow hall will appear wider.

In practical terms, a wooden floor is quickly and easily swept and mopped down, which may need to be done frequently to keep this heavy traffic area well-maintained. Wooden boards can also be limed,

This blue hall wall
changes color as day
passes into night. In
daylight it is a strong and
impressive shade that is
fresh and vibrant; at night
the color becomes more
intense but muted and
rich.

stained or painted to change their appearance. To achieve a simple hint of color in what might otherwise be a cold or bare vestibule, apply a wash of dilute latex paint on the walls sealed with a matt varnish or similar finish.

Not all hallways are straight; some disappear around a corner or bend, others may be cut off by, or disappear up, a staircase. To continue the flow and feeling of a passageway, use a similar color or type of floor covering and wall finish to direct not only the eye, but also the senses, along it.

INTRODUCING LIGHT AND AIR

A hallway should be as well lit as possible. In a long hallway, use a mirror or paint the wall at the end with a pale, reflective color to bounce back light and give a feeling of space. It is also more reassuring to be able to see the end of a corridor and gauge the length at a glance, getting an overall feeling for the environment. Keep hallway and entrance colors fresh but not over-stimulating. For example, a bright red could be unsettling and overbearing, while a neutral oatmeal or off-white shade would be bright and clean by daylight but softer and more relaxing in the evening, by electric light.

To bring extra natural light to a hallway or front door area, which is often windowless, you might consider putting a plain or opaque glass panel above the door in the style of a Georgian fan light. This upper window will allow light to fall down and along a narrow corridor and, in addition, may be reflected and doubled with the use of a mirror. The glass for an over door window should be reinforced and well secured for safety reasons. To bring a touch of color to an entrance, the glass could be stained so that the daylight that passes through will become tinted.

If the hall is in a single-storey building or a top floor that has access to the roof, you may be able to introduce yet more light by placing skylight windows into the ceiling. These overhead windows will allow pools of light to fall along the length of the corridor and, depending on the size and shape of the windows, it may also create a constantly changing pattern of light that will decorate the walls and floor. These overhead windows need not open, so a dome-shaped inset rather than a standard window could be an interesting and unusual option.

There are a number of other ways in which you can coax light from levels or windows above to penetrate the lower hallway and to brighten the stairs themselves. Replace dense side panels or thick balustrades with fine but sturdy high-tension cable or narrow metal spindles, which provide safety and support but do not cut out the light. Alternatively, paint dark wood panelling white or a similar, light-reflective color to help bounce back any available light.

A small electric light with a low wattage or long-life bulb can be left on in a hallway throughout an evening or if the house is left empty. The light is not only a comforting beacon, it can also make the house appear lived in, which may help deter burglars. The symbol of the light—like a flame, fire or torch—also reflects warmth and vitality within the home.

As well as the welcoming nocturnal light and the use of an over door glass panel to allow extra natural daylight into the area, there may be doors that lead off the hall or entrance way that could be altered to increase the flow of light. For example, if a door leads to a

room that does not have an intimate or private use, such as a dining room or kitchen, then consider replacing the panels in the upper half of the door with reinforced glass that is either plain or etched. Lower panels are usually best left as wood or similar hard material to avoid damage by kicking or knocking. Also there is usually little free flow of light at lower levels due to furniture and the fact that windows on outer walls are generally placed above waist level.

In a hall or doorway area where there are windows but the view is unpleasant or distracting, think about changing the glass from clear to opaque or even glass bricks, which will permit the light to flow through in a softly diffused way and at the same time conceal the outlook. Opaque glass will also give you privacy from the eyes of passers-by and is easy to wipe clean with a damp cloth or specific glass cleaner. These more permanent shields are easier to maintain than cotton or voile net curtains, which need to be taken down, washed, dried, and re-hung. In areas where space is limited, a blind or obscure glass will also save valuable space that might otherwise be taken up by the folds of a curtain.

A PLACE OF WELCOME

As well as being a practical place to wipe, clean or take off shoes, and hang coats, the area immediately by the front door will also be the place to greet and bid farewell to guests. To shield the rest of an open-plan room from cold air let in by the door or the glances of casual visitors, you may like to create a screen that forms a barrier between the door and the rest of the room.

The screen can be permanent, such as a built-in bookcase or cabinet, or lightweight like a folding wood or bamboo screen. Even a tab-top curtain suspended from a bamboo rod and attached to hooks screwed into the ceiling will create a protective and attractive decorative layer and give the impression that the main thoroughfare and bustle of the doorway is removed from the rest of the room, where a feeling of calm and tranquility is required.

The way into your home can also be made inviting by placing a flower or plant on a shelf or table by the doorway. In the evening, light an incense joss stick or scented candle to perfume the air; it will instantly create a feeling of peace and calm. This initial arrival zone is important because it sets the mood and tempo as soon as someone comes through the door.

For example, if a weary commuter arrives home from the office having battled with traffic and bad weather, this is the first place where the process of relaxation and unwinding will begin. Similarly, if someone else has dragged shopping bags home and coped with the check-out lines in shops and supermarkets, this is the area where the car keys are put down and the bags unloaded with a feeling of weariness. The atmosphere at this point should be as welcoming, calming, and familiar as possible.

As well as making the main entrance to your home hospitable and practical, look at the entrances into each room. If you have a corridor off which other rooms are accessible, leave some if not all the doors to the other rooms ajar. This assists the flow of light and air and provides the passer-by a welcoming glimpse into the rooms.

To someone who is new to your home, open doors are reassuring and give the impression that there is nothing to hide. If doors are closed, it may create a feeling that there are restrictions to the meeting. It is also difficult to relax fully if you are unsure of your environment and hidden spaces behind closed door are unknown territories.

The staircase is set in between two walls but because the top is open and the walls are white there is no feeling of being constricted or claustrophobic.

It can be important for your comfort to feel that there is an openness and free flow of Chi around the rooms or spaces within your home. But there are also times when solitude and personal time and space are needed, so make sure there are places available where this can be achieved.

The way into your home—whether it be inner-city apartment or country house—is important as it establishes the tone and feeling of your domain. To arrive into a calm and tranquil entrance will make you feel relieved, revived, and relaxed, away from the bustle and stress of the outside world, which you have left locked behind the door you have just closed.

EATING

INCREASINGLY, EATING AND COOKING PLACES HAVE BECOME ADJACENT OR JOINED. THE FUNCTIONS OF FOOD PREPARATION AND DINING ARE NO LONGER ISOLATED BUT HAVE BECOME PARTS OF THE SAME LIVING SPACE. THE BREAKFAST BAR THAT LINKS KITCHEN AND DINING AREA OR A KNOCKED THROUGH OPENING BETWEEN THE TWO AREAS ARE NOW COMMON FEATURES IN PURPOSE-BUILT OR ADAPTED MODERN LIVING SPACE. THIS DOUBLING-UP OF USES USUALLY MEANS THAT THE KITCHEN/EATING AREA BECOMES ONE OF THE MOST USED AND COMMUNAL SPACES IN THE HOUSE, AND THEREFORE THE BUSIEST AND MOST DIFFICULT IN WHICH TO MAINTAIN ORDER.

ACCESS BETWEEN THE KITCHEN AND DINING AREA MUST BE FREE AND UNHINDERED, NOT ONLY FOR EASE OF MOVEMENT AND SAFETY WHEN CARRYING PLATES, GLASSES, OR HOT DISHES, BUT ALSO FOR VISUAL CONTINUITY. THIS CAN ALSO BE ENHANCED BY THE USE OF THE SAME DECORATING MATERIALS AND COLORS THROUGHOUT. AN ISLAND UNIT THAT CAN BE REACHED FROM BOTH AREAS CAN BE USEFUL FOR PLACING DISHES ON AND STACKING USED PLATES AFTER THE MEAL. A LOW WALL OF STORAGE UNITS CAN ALSO FORM A SIMILAR, PRACTICAL BUT DEFINITIVE DIVIDE BETWEEN THE TWO AREAS AND THEIR SEPARATE FUNCTIONS.

THE DINING SECTION OF THE ROOM MAY BE REQUIRED TO FULFILL A NUMBER OF ROLES FROM CHILDREN'S BREAKFAST ZONE TO ADULT'S ENTERTAINING VENUE, WHICH WILL MEAN THAT THE LIGHTING AND DECORATION HAS TO BE ADAPTABLE. THE KITCHEN TABLE MAY ALSO BE AN AREA WHERE HOMEWORK IS DONE AS WELL AS RECREATIONAL PAINTING AND PASTIMES.

PLACES

ABOVE: In simple surroundings the textures and colors of mats, plates, and cutlery become a focal point on the table.

LEFT: A view of a garden or the landscape beyond is a pleasant and calming focal point for an eating place.

This multi-use space echoes the layout of the Japanese tea house—an authentic example of a Zen style interior—where lightweight sliding walls are all that separate one area from another. The main space is used for sitting and taking tea and may be utilized for sleeping or resting as well. This uncomplicated style can be a useful source of inspiration when planning the scheme and style of your eating place.

In the Western home, the kitchen is often the center of domestic life with washing, food preparation, and eating taking place in the same space and often at the same time. With so many requirements focused on one room, careful planning is important not just to make everything fit in and be workable but also to avoid the place becoming uncomfortably crowded and untidy.

The first stage in any re-organization or re-design of the kitchen and dining area should be done once you have completed the streamlining and editing process. Taking into consideration the Zen doctrine of possessions being burdens, try to eliminate what is not necessary and neatly store things that are seldom used in less readily accessible places, leaving the accessible storage for things that are used regularly.

CREATING A UTILITY AREA

Although in a pure Zen household possessions would be minimal—a sleeping mat, neck roll, bowl for rice, chopsticks, bamboo steamer and a cup—the average, labor-saving modern kitchen requires space for many machines such as dishwashers, food processors, microwaves, toaster, refrigerators, freezers, and extractor fans. To achieve any semblance of Zen-inspired tranquility and spaciousness, as many of these appliances as possible should be concealed or made to disappear.

If your kitchen/eating space is very large, you may consider annexing a section off at one end of the main or open-plan room to create a separate utility space. Putting the larger and noisier machines in a walled-off area away from the rest of the room will also keep noise levels down. Laundry and even dishwashing facilities could be located in the utility area, keeping the heat and moisture that these types of machines generate away from the main working and dining areas. A certain amount of storage for bulky items such as bottles, cans and newspapers for recycling can also be located here, as can toxic

Low cupboards on two walls of this room mean that other surfaces can be kept clear and that plates, linens, and candles can be stored close at hand. This makes setting the table a less time-consuming and laborious task.

bleaches and cleaners that are best kept as far away from the food preparation area as possible.

If creating a specific utility space is not feasible, try to make the appliances and storage spaces as innocuous and unobtrusive as possible. By using matching panels or uniform fronts, the gadgets and machines can be made to appear featureless and part of a wall. A continuous run of identical units or matching cupboards will give a feeling of harmony and consistency that can make a small space appear to be larger.

Many kitchen companies now supply false doors to be fixed on to the existing white fronts of dishwashers and washing machines so that they appear the same as the rest of the built-in units. For this uniform look, make sure that your dishwasher or other appliances have controls that are recessed into the upper, interior rim of the machine, rather than the outer face, so that they can be easily accessed. In unfitted kitchens, or those already fitted, disguise the appliances behind a simple blind or curtain or behind a false door made of tongue-and-groove panelling, whichever best suits the overall scheme of the room.

A simple but effective way of creating a false wall behind which both appliances and shelves are concealed, is with lightweight sliding doors. These can be made from white, handmade paper sandwiched between lightweight sheets of Plexiglas designed to protect the paper as well as giving a practical, wipe-clean surface, but are sufficiently portable to slide on fine runners fixed to the ceiling and floor. A similar piece of camouflage can be achieved with light bamboo blinds screwed into the ceiling so that the blinds can be raised to give ready access to the shelves of storage behind. But when the shelves are not in use the blinds can be lowered to form an attractive, lightweight screen of bamboo in front of the shelving.

When plumbing and wiring appliances into cabinets or behind close-fitting fronts, do ensure there is adequate ventilation so that heat and steam can be ducted away rather than left to build up in a confined space. The resulting condensation can settle on machine parts, causing rust or other damage. It may also be worth putting the larger, heavier appliances on wheel-lock roller bases so that they can subsequently be easily removed from the casing for maintenance, repairs, or general cleaning purposes.

MAKING THE MOST OF SHELVES AND CUPBOARDS

Where possible, leave the upper areas of the walls clear of built-in units as this will add to a feeling of space and openness. This is important in small kitchens where upper wall storage, especially with solid doors, can make the walls appear to close in. Upper cupboards with open shelves, and to some extent glass-fronted cupboards, help reduce the feeling of crowding and simultaneously supply some useful shelf space.

Open shelving should be primarily utilized to store items that are used on a regular basis because, without the protection of solid or glass doors, the items displayed and the shelves themselves will be subject to the effects of condensation and the general build-up of grease and dust that can accumulate in a kitchen. Also, to achieve visual harmony on open shelves, display the items rather than shoving them back on the shelf haphazardly.

Construct lower units and work areas so that they are at a height that is easy and comfortable for those who stand and work at them. If there are tall and small inhabitants in your home, you may find it a good idea to have work top areas at different heights. It is important for those who cook and prepare food frequently, not to stoop or stretch to have access to the chopping board or stove because this may cause back problems and muscle aches in the neck, shoulder, and arm regions, which will cause tension and be stressful and wearing.

Other things that are used frequently during the day and are stored on the work surface near the food preparation area, should be kept in similar or identical containers so that they become a unit rather than a discordant jumble of jars and cans. As with items for display (see pages 138–47), the more understated and minimal the containers and their location, the more important their quality and finish becomes.

When there is little else around to distract the eye, your focus is attracted to whatever there is to view, so that a row of three polished steel storage jars in an otherwise clutter-free kitchen, will in themselves become a point of interest, so choose even these simple items with great care. Also, when the background color scheme is neutral and neat, any item of color—a red bowl or a sunflower—takes on an increased importance. The plain background will also concentrate attention on the food served such as the vivid colors and textures of carrot, red pepper, and cabbage leaves.

A lightweight table and chairs can be moved towards the window for meals during the summer, or further in to the heart of the room for warmth and comfort in the winter.

With produce and utensils that are stored out of sight it is advisable to locate them nearest to the point where they are most likely to be used. For example, keep the food processor in a cupboard near the area of work surface and electric socket where it is most often employed. Keep sharp knives and chopping boards near the sink or stove so that chopping and peeling can be done near the pots or woks that the food will be cooked in or the trash bin where the waste matter will be disposed. This planning and analysis of daily routine can save a great deal of time and effort and leave scope for relaxing, meditating, and maintaining a calm outlook.

CHOOSING SURFACE MATERIALS

With reference to the Zen-inspired idea of a person's contact with nature, decorate the eating area with natural materials, such as stone and wood, used in conjunction with the more contemporary surfaces of stainless steel and glass. Wood, with modern water- and stain-resistant finishes, can be utilized in most areas from the floor to work

Only items that are regularly used should be left on display in a kitchen, otherwise they need to be frequently washed or wiped down to remove any deposits of dust or grease.

These lightweight sliding
screens of hand-made
paper sandwiched
between Plexiglas,
camouflage shelves of
ingredients, machines,
and crockery and create
a continuous, almost
featureless, wall at the
end of the kitchen.

tops, seating, tables, and shelves. By using one material, such as wood, for the majority of the interior you can create a simplicity and unity that is pleasing and calming to live with.

In areas where a lot of water is present or where heat can be excessive or temperatures extreme, such as around the sink and stove, use materials that are more resilient. Stainless steel or natural materials such as slate and granite are all useful in these conditions. Marble, too, is worth considering because as it is a cold surface it is ideal for making pastry and preparing fish or poultry. Think, too, of insetting steel, as in a double sink and drainer, or an enduring marble pastry slab into the layout of the kitchen at the specific points where they are required.

Other materials that are worth thinking about include ceramic or terracotta tiles, zinc sheeting, and in certain places copper. Wicker baskets and drawers can also be useful for storing vegetables and fruit. The open basketwork weave allows air to circulate, which will prevent the contents from becoming moldy due to pressure or bruising, which can occur on the airless base of a solid or sealed container.

When choosing the materials and paints to use in eating places and food preparation areas, be careful to read the instructions, or ask the advice of the retailer, to ensure that there are no toxic contents or finishes in the products you are using.

Simple colors and a limited number of materials and surfaces means that it is easy to touch up, repair or repaint the room, giving it a thorough spring cleaning or a fresh coat of paint every year or so. Similarly, if the surfaces are kept clean and devoid of unnecessary clutter such as storage jars, spice jars and chopping boards they will also be quick and simple to wipe down on a daily basis and after each time you prepare food or cook.

The kitchen, where food is prepared and cooked, is one of the most important areas to keep clean and hygienic and should be totally free of toxins and pollutants. It may take a while to adjust to putting things away after they are used, but in the long term it becomes part of a routine and the advantage is that you save time overall.

PLANNING THE DECOR

To start planning your decorative scheme, select simple and sturdy but stylish furniture that will last and make a good base on which to build. Choose a shape of table to suit not only your needs but also the shape of the space available for it. Round tables tend to give more seating in a small space, but in a narrow or linear room, an oblong table can be more aesthetically pleasing. Tables with inset panels or fold-down flaps are useful because they can be reduced or enlarged as needed. To keep in touch with the feeling of harmony and balance that Zen favors, use chairs of the same design and color and in equal numbers on each side of the table.

Where possible, make the most of any natural light that comes into the room or rooms. Keep the windows simply dressed, and to maximize the light, paint the frames in pale or white paint. It is worth remembering that when in full working order, the kitchen or cooking end of the room can be steamy and greasy so any soft furnishings such as curtains should be easy to wash and re-hang. A roller blind is a simple yet useful window shield: it can be stored out of harm's way in a tight furl at the top of the window or rolled down to block out the darkness of night or an unpleasant view.

An island block can be a useful feature not only because it provides extra work surface but also because it provides a barrier between the food preparation and eating areas of the kitchen.

LEFT: The cooking and preparation area of this kitchen is secreted behind the floating wall, but there is still easy access from the kitchen to the dining area although it is not clearly visible.

RIGHT: For more formal dining you may want to slide a screen over the kitchen or close a door on it completely so that the steam and smells of the meal do not invade the dining space.

Reflective surfaces such as steel, and to some extent pale, glazed tiles, will also help reflect natural light, but be careful that they are not in direct, powerful sunlight, which might cause harsh reflected light to dazzle and be temporarily blinding. Mirror, although reflective, is seldom used in a kitchen because of glare and the problems of reflection, but in a dining area, a mirror that reflects the food being served is believed by some to indicate wealth and signify the doubling of the food on the table.

Keeping the area around windows and doors free of entanglements such as curtains also means that they are easy to open and close. Open windows and doors will help with natural air circulation, which will in turn ventilate these busy rooms and remove steam, condensation, or cooking smells. When it is not possible to open windows and doors, or if there aren't many or large enough ones to create a good through flow of air, then an electric fan or filter positioned immediately over the stove will help to freshen it. Good air circulation is important not only for the general atmosphere in the room but also for the movement of Chi energy.

LIGHTING

The type of lighting and its positioning will be instrumental in creating the right mood and atmosphere for the eating space. In the area where the storage, preparation, and cooking of food takes place, choose lighting from the task category (see page 65). Where cupboards are deep, at the lower level or in a shaded part of the room, you may find small in-cupboard lights especially useful. This type of lighting can be fixed to a push-in switch in the door so that when the door is opened the spring on the light switch is released and the light automatically comes on. Conversely, when the door is closed, the switch is compressed and the light goes out.

Over a stove and area of work surface where hot pans and woks and sharp knives are in use, arrange the light so that it gives a good, clear and shadow-free illumination. If lights are positioned behind the person working, a shadow falls across the work surface, which means that the tasks being undertaken are not clearly seen and so may cause accidents. Other lighting in the kitchen should be ambient but of sufficient strength to give a clear view of all working and walking areas.

Around the dining area, install a specific light focused on the table with a dimmer switch attached. This light may need to be capable of providing sufficient illumination for close work such as reading, writing and drawing. But when dimmed, it can also supply a low-level glow which can be used in conjunction with a two- or three- layer arrangement in the rest of the room.

The layer arrangement may include a couple of wall-mounted lights, also on a dimmer switch, which can be used to re-enforce the strength of the pendant light. It may also replace the central light by providing a more subtle, less direct ambient light for a dinner party or more formal evening meal. To endorse the subtle lighting even more, introduce some decorative lighting in the form of candles or a small oil lamp, placed on the table, side tables or cleared work surfaces.

By turning off all lighting in the kitchen, that end of the room can fall into shadow and out of sight so that the emphasis of the room is solely on the dining or eating area. Playing, or as some would say painting, with light in this way can be rewarding, enabling you to create the right feeling and setting for whatever meals you are serving.

This extension to the back of a period house has created a light, spacious, contemporary dining area with a view to the garden and easy access to the kitchen, which is through the opening to the left.

ZEN-INSPIRED DETAILS

The positioning of moveable furniture such as the table and chairs is a good way of making the most of the different aspects of the room. If you have windows or French doors overlooking an attractive garden, you may wish to make the most of the view and contact with nature by placing the table and chairs so that they are near not only the natural light from the window but also the panorama.

As advocated by Zen thinking, watching the seasonal changes, the flowering of plants and shrubs, and the daily activity of birds, butterflies and other wild life, gives you a chance to be in touch with your surroundings and be aware of the passing of time. However, in the winter you may want to distance yourself a little from the view and coldness of the room's edge by moving the table and chairs nearer to the warmth of the center.

Lighting is not the only way to change the feeling and spirit of the dining table. As the eye and mind become focused, the color and arrangement of the food being served becomes important. This in turn draws attention to the way the table is laid.

As Zen-inspired rooms tend to be decorated in a minimal and pale scheme you may like to use the china and table linen to bring color and a change of emphasis to your table top. Select plates and napkins to complement the type of food you are serving. For example, a fresh stir-fry of vegetables and rice would look especially appetizing and in harmony in hand-thrown porcelain bowls in pale green, speckled blue, or earthy tones of brown.

For a romantic evening meal by candlelight or dimmed light, red or deep pink napkins and tablecloth add a touch of heat or even passion to the meal. For breakfast, a zesty yellow or green is invigorating and for a dinner party where there are many guests, a simple setting of fresh white napkins and plain white china accentuate the feelings of cleanliness, space, and calmness.

The eating space is worth taking some time over. By achieving a spacious and orderly layout, you will quickly find the everyday activities of cooking and eating become less demanding and stressful, and consequently something that is far easier and more enjoyable to do.

LIVING

AS WITH EATING PLACES, THE LIVING AREA OF A HOME ALSO HAS TO CATER TO A NUMBER OF DIFFERENT USES. THE MAIN LIVING ROOM IS NOT ONLY A PLACE TO SIT IN AND ENJOY THE COMPANY OF FRIENDS AND FAMILY, IT MAY ALSO NEED TO BE A SOLITARY CHAMBER WHERE YOU TAKE TIME ALONE TO UNWIND AND ENJOY THE PEACE, COMFORT, AND TRANQUILITY THAT SURROUNDS YOU.

THE ROOM IS ALSO LIKELY TO DOUBLE AS AN ENTERTAINMENT SPACE ACCOMPANIED BY THE VERY UN-ŻEN ITEMS OF TELEVISION, HI-FI AND OTHER ELECTRONIC ACCESSORIES. IF THE KITCHEN AREA OF THE APARTMENT OR HOUSE IS SMALL, PART OF THE LIVING AREA MAY ALSO BE USED FOR DINING, WHICH WILL ALSO HAVE TO BE CONSIDERED IN THE GENERAL LAYOUT.

IF THE ROOM IS TALL, THERE MAY BE THE POSSIBILITY OF CREATING A MEZZANINE OR BALCONY AREA WHERE ONE OR TWO OF THE FUNCTIONS OF THE ROOM COULD BE LOCATED, LEAVING MORE FREE SPACE ON THE LOWER LEVEL. MAKE THIS UPPER AREA SECURE WITH RAILINGS OR POLES OF STEEL AND HIGH-TENSION STEEL WIRE. THIS ALSO HAS THE BENEFIT OF ALLOWING AN UNOBSTRUCTED FLOW OF LIGHT AND PROVIDES A PROTECTIVE BOUNDARY.

A living space may need to be subdivided into smaller, inner rooms, so that there are different aspects and areas to cater for various needs.

REINFORCED GLASS WALLS OR OPAQUE PANELS COULD ALSO BE USED. THESE WOULD BE IDEAL IF THE UPPER AREA BECAME THE ENTERTAINMENT ZONE BECAUSE THE STRENGTHENED GLASS WOULD GIVE SOME SOUND INSULATION WITHOUT CUTTING OFF THE LIGHT OR MAKING THE MEZZANINE AREA ISOLATED. IF THE UPPER AREA IS SMALL, THEN THE GLASS OR RAILINGS WILL MAKE IT SEEM MORE SPACIOUS THAN A SOLID WALL.

PLACES

ORGANIZING THE SPACE

When planning the layout of the living space, try to imagine a number of smaller rooms within the room. For example, if there is a fireplace, this is often the focus of the space and chairs and sofas can be organized around it to create a group meeting area or the center of the room. The backs of the sofas and chairs will create a barrier to anything behind them, creating a series of "walls" around the inner space.

A dining table is usually a large and dominant feature and, like the sofas, one that takes up space as well as creating a "wall" or barrier.

Even if the table has a glass top, which gives the feeling of being light and airy, the table itself creates a physical wall. Site these two prominent pieces of furniture and primary functions first then, in the remaining space, arrange the other "rooms" or sub-sections.

If the area is large enough there may be space to identify and establish a meditative area. This area could be a window seat, floor cushions, or a chair that can be used by a person who wants to read or be separate from the group area of sofas and armchairs. This does not need to be a fixed space, but one that can be identified and used

This clean, open space offers an upholstered sofa for relaxing and reading on, as well as a low bench and table where a broadsheet newspaper can be spread out or homework done.

when needed. The television and music section forms the entertainment zone and can be part of the group area or set back in a separate space so that this activity can also be enjoyed independently.

A study or desk area is also useful in the living room. Ensure there are shelves close to the desk so that files or books can be at hand. A desk is often a magnet for bits of paper, bills awaiting payment and odd pencils, pens and stationery which, if left disorganized, turn to clutter. So endeavor to keep the desk neat by having a drawer or box for pens and pencils and a file or tray for papers. The telephone, answering

The fireplace provides a focus to this sitting area. The patterned rug placed beneath the chairs also helps to define the space; the angular, corner shape of the seats also creates a safe and enclosed feeling.

Z
E
N

machine, and other machines such as a computer may also need to be placed here, which will create a work environment. To avoid work or business matters intruding into an area of relaxation and calmness, a lightweight screen or even a desk built into a closet, whose deep doors are lined with shelves and filing spaces, will keep the two conflicting criteria apart.

To cope with all these functions in one space, keep things simple and minimal. Where possible, conceal unsightly machines such as the television and music center with all their associated wiring and knobs in a cabinet or behind a discreet panel or door. This can then be opened for viewing or disc changing but closed when the machine is not in use. As with kitchen units concealing appliances, the enclosure should be ventilated, either by small drilled holes at the back or by a cooling system.

If space is limited, use built-in furniture to make the most of every available inch. For example, extend the hearth of a raised fireplace on either side to create a continuous bench. The lower area can be boxed-in and used as storage space with access through a hinged lid. When closed, cover the lid with a cushion to provide a seat. A box bench built over ugly, lower wall piping will disguise the plumbing and create a low seat or display surface. In a bay or curved window, build up the area under the sill to make a window seat or even a desk with storage space beneath.

FLOORS FOR LIVING WITH

Unlike the kitchen, the living area has more space for softness and comfort because the hygiene requirements are less stringent. The floor covering in this area can be soft and more textural. In a pure Zen interior, the floor would most likely be of wood covered with tatami matting, but for those who find that warmth and comfort are important for relaxation and tranquility then golden colored coir, sisal, jute, and seagrass natural floor coverings or one of the several styles of pure wool carpet that are woven to appear like a natural fiber, will provide a soft and comfortable layer underfoot.

In Zen style homes, outdoor shoes are left by the door when entering the house and replaced by soft indoor shoes or thick socks. This is not only more comfortable and better for your feet but with

ABOVE: The raised area around the fireplace creates two long benches which, with a little extra padding provided by cushions, becomes a place to perch and chat or lounge and read.

natural floor coverings it is practical too. Small bits of stone or grit caught in the tread or sole of a shoe or even high heels can damage the weave and cut the fibers, eventually harming the surface. Also, pale colored floors, whether pine, colored washed wood or natural matting, will last longer and remain cleaner if they are only walked on by clean, soft soles.

Strip and sand existing hardwood floors to remove dark stains or varnish. Stripping over a large area is best done with a rented machine, which is like an upright vacuum cleaner, as covering a large area with a chemical remover is messy and the smell and effect of the chemicals unpleasant for anyone who is working with it. If there are any cracks or gaping joins, fill them and finally seal with a wax or light, transparent gloss or matt sealant.

Wool or cotton mats placed on a wooden floor will bring comfort and quietness underfoot. The positions of the mats can also identify the different areas within the room. For example, a mat laid in front of a window and away from the main furniture becomes an island place, and could be where solitary meditation or reading takes place. A hearth rug in front of the fire, around which the sofas and armchairs are arranged indicates the group sitting area. A large mat placed under the dining table will not only be useful to catch crumbs and debris, which can be carried out on the mat and shaken off outdoors, but will further identify the eating area.

THE IMPORTANCE OF COMFORT

If you opt for white walls and keep to the minimalist, uncluttered approach then it is important the room is well supplied with heating as well as ventilation. A stark room can feel cooler than a cluttered one at the same temperature because psychologically there is nothing to protect you, no barrier between the enveloping whiteness and cold and the body. A comfortably warm room also enables you to wear fewer and looser clothes, which makes the body, and subsequently the spirit, freer, less restricted and more able to relax.

In a room that is well heated and ventilated, or even a room that gets regular and strong heat from the sun, it may be necessary to place bowls of water to keep moisture in the air. A dry atmosphere can dehydrate people sitting in the room and may, after some time, make their skin and eyes feel uncomfortably dry and scratchy. Lack of moisture combined with excessive warmth may also induce a feeling of lethargy, sleepiness, or irritability.

Furniture and paintings may also suffer from over dryness as much as they do from damp so the right level of moisture in the air is important. If bowls of water do not seem adequate, consider purchasing a conventional humidifier from a department store or shop, and this will dispense humidity as and when it is required.

Even if you have just a few pieces of furniture these should be chosen for comfort and support. Ergonomically designed chairs that support the lower lumbar region and shoulders and do not subject the backs of the thighs to undue pressure are ideal. A foot stool or ottoman can be used to raise the feet and take the pressure off the legs and ankles, which also improves blood circulation. Many great thinkers from Mahatma Gandhi to Thomas Jefferson have found the reclining position beneficial from which to work.

A deep, well-stuffed sofa is an inviting piece of furniture to stretch out on, but for children it may be necessary to supply small scatter

These brightly colored and unusually shaped chairs not only provide a place to sit but add color and interest in an otherwise plainly decorated room. The pink tinge on the petals of the amaryllis also highlights the red of the chair.

The extended wooden hearth creates a low display area as well as a narrow bench on which to perch. It also emphasizes the small fireplace and provides a horizontal break along the expanse of plain white wall.

cushions to support them comfortably at the edge of the seat or to wedge them in so that they don't slip or fall over. With upholstered furniture, make sure the covers are removable and washable: this is essential if the fabrics are pale or white. General wear and tear will cause the fabrics to become soiled or greasy and for a perfect Zen interior the covers should be pristine.

ACHIEVING THE PERFECT BALANCE

The positioning of furniture will affect not only the appearance of the room but also the flow of Chi and the ease with which you can move around. Avoid creating a boxed-in area with sofas and chairs. Although the group seating around the fireplace or other center of focus in the room should be intimate, there should be a person-size space between each piece of furniture so that people can enter and leave with ease. Occasional tables should not be hazardous objects, they are best sited next to the piece of furniture that they will be used with, say beside the arm of an easy chair or sofa. Small, low tables in isolated

spaces not only appear to be remote but can also be forgotten and—even worse—tripped over.

A clear passageway between the door to the room and the main window will encourage the movement of Chi, which is important for the feeling of well-being. Stagnant Chi can lead to lethargy, sadness, and low energy levels. This negative Chi affects not only people but also plants and any other living thing in the room. You may find that flowers wilt and leaves become lackluster where stagnant Chi is present.

For a harmonious living room, the shapes of the room, furniture, and decorations should be balanced. If you have square, boxy seats, counteract the squareness with a small, round coffee table. If you have a run of long tall windows, place a round rug or mat in front of the middle one or cover it with a blind with a circle painted or appliquéd onto it.

Also think of textures in this way. Too many smooth surfaces can be bland, so put a rough linen or raw silk cushion on a chair upholstered in a smooth, chintz cotton or a hand-woven straw mat on a glass table, to bring contrast and interest to the room.

Although purists in the Zen philosophy deem possessions to be burdens, a few, well-chosen pieces will add to the feeling of hominess of a room which, if left undressed, may appear institutional and unsettling. As there will be only a few specially chosen pieces on show they will be examined more closely and be a focus of attention, so put a lot of thought into their selection. What you may like to do is follow the Asian tradition of storing your precious or beautiful pieces of art or pottery in a display cabinet and change the arrangement of display on a weekly or seasonal basis so that there is variety and interest in the room.

Flowers are the ultimate changeable accessory. The infinite varieties offer such a range of color and shape that there could be a different stem or flower in the room every week. The scent can also fill the room so use seasonal scented flowers such as narcissi, roses, mimosa, and jasmine to bring joy with their color and aroma. When flowers are out of season or should you wish to ring the changes, a bowl of water with choice pebbles at the bottom or a wooden plate covered with pine cones, or seed pods can be equally attractive. Even kitchen spices such as star anise, cloves, cinnamon bark, and nutmeg,

ZEN

LEFT: The lighting, on fine steel wires, is adjustable so that the emphasis of the pools of light from each bulb can be relocated if the table is moved.

RIGHT: This two level room provides a lower, general entertaining space and a smaller, upper area with a table for paperwork or quiet reading.

can be arranged in a small dish to bring aroma, texture, and color to side tables, shelves, or a windowsill.

Use color, too, to play its part in creating the right aura or atmosphere. Yellow is said to be good for dispersing stagnant Chi energy and red is associated with fire and warmth. It is also regarded as an auspicious color, except for hot-tempered people who should keep the color to a minimum in their environment. Also make use of others colors in small but significant amounts. For example, the Zen-style uncluttered living room may look a little bleak as winter draws in and the long dark mornings and evenings seem to sap you of energy and enthusiasm. A couple of red or strong pink cushions and a throw on a sofa or chair create a feeling of warmth and help increase the energy in the room.

LIGHTING

Lighting in a living space should be variable to suit the moods and tasks encountered within it. As with the eating area, lighting on several levels can be useful. In a large room, floor lamps may be helpful and add to the mid-level of lighting in areas not adequately covered by wall lights.

The right choice of lampshades can also be vital in creating the right mood. A richly colored or thickly covered shade will cut back the amount of light transmitted, directing it downward and upward rather than as a general glow. Paper lampshades, made from heat-treated paper and supported by a frame that keeps the bulb well away from the paper, give a soft and diffuse glow, which can be made to appear even warmer by using a tinted bulb with just a hint of pink, yellow, or gold.

Good lighting is essential when you are planning a working area in your home. For areas where reading and paperwork may take place, have eye-level task lights at hand. A small adjustable desk lamp may suit the study area as its head can be directed on to the desk top for paper work. An adjustable floor light or a side-table lamp will help those reading a book, magazine, or newspaper on the sofa or in an easy chair.

Use focus lighting to highlight objects or works of art. Over a calligraphy panel or painting, for example, a small strip picture-light will emphasize the color and content, especially in the evening if the surrounding area is left dark. The spotlight will give the piece of art it is highlighting impact and importance. Light a glass object displayed on a glass shelf with a fine optic fiber light, which will make the object appear to glow and even to float rather than sit on the shelf.

Natural daylight may also need to be regulated, especially if you have large windows. Direct sunlight can be powerful and will not only bleach and fade flooring and upholstery but may also be too intense for the eye to cope with without squinting or shielding the eyes. Rather than thick or voluptuous curtains, louver blinds are effective and easily adjusted so that just the right amount of light comes into the room. They also provide privacy by covering the window but without blocking all the light.

Although large, uncovered windows are fine overlooking a flower, filled garden and blue sky during a sunny day, they may appear as big, blank black spaces at night. This dark outlook, and the lack of a barrier between the inner and outer worlds, can be unsettling and uncomfortable, so some form of window dressing is advisable in most rooms. A white roller blind, or blind in the same color as the walls or window surrounds will fit neatly against the window and can make it appear to be a continuation of the wall. Bamboo or textured blinds or fabric panels give an element of decoration and warmth as well as obscuring the dark.

Fitting so many requirements into one space can be complicated, but with edited down books, artifacts and possessions, a carefully constructed plan and a will to be disciplined and ordered, it can be an enjoyable and fulfilling space—and one that you will be happy to return to day after day.

Overhead light pours in through glass panels and creates a feeling of being outdoors although you are inside. The plentiful supply of light also encourages plant growth like the curtain of green along the end wall.

SLEEPING

ON AVERAGE, WE SPEND A THIRD OF OUR LIVES IN BED, WHICH MAKES THE ROOM WHERE WE REST, USUALLY THE BEDROOM, ONE OF THE MOST IMPORTANT BUT LEAST PUBLIC PLACES IN THE HOUSE. IN WESTERN CULTURES, THE BEDROOM IS USUALLY A PRIVATE AND PERSONAL SPACE WHERE WE CLOSE THE DOOR, SHUT OUT THE REST OF THE WORLD, AND SEEK SOME INDIVIDUAL HAVEN. THE LAYOUT AND DECORATION OF THE ROOM THEN ARE EXTREMELY INFLUENTIAL IN REACHING THAT ZEN-LIKE STATE OF TRANQUILITY, WHICH WILL ENABLE THE MIND AND BODY TO RELAX.

HARMONY IS A VITAL ELEMENT IN A BEDROOM AND TO ACHIEVE IT, IT IS USEFUL TO LOOK TO THE EASTERN BALANCED FORCES OF YIN AND YANG. THESE TWO FORCES ARE ILLUSTRATED AS A CIRCLE SUB-DIVIDED INTO TWO TEAR-DROP SHAPES, ONE BLACK AND ONE WHITE. IN ITS ENTIRETY, THE YIN AND YANG CIRCLE ILLUSTRATES THE BELIEF THAT ALL PHENOMENA ARE MANIFESTATIONS OF ONE INFINITY.

WITHIN THE CIRCLE, THE WHITE AREA REPRESENTS YANG, WHICH IS THE LIGHTER, BRIGHTER ENERGY, AND THE DARKER OR BLACK AREA, THE YIN ENERGY. WITHIN EACH OF THE DIVISIONS THERE IS A TINY PINPOINT OF THE OPPOSITE'S ENERGY, WHICH SHOWS THAT NOTHING IS EVER TOTALLY YIN OR ABSOLUTELY YANG AND THAT THERE IS A SMALL AMOUNT OF THE OPPOSITE'S CHARACTER WITHIN EACH EXTREME. YANG'S ASSOCIATIONS ON THE WHITE SIDE ARE THE SUN, WARMTH, LIGHT, ACTIVITY, MOVEMENT, AND LIFE. YIN, THE DARKER SIDE, IS ASSOCIATED WITH THE EARTH, THE WINTER, COOLNESS, DARK, STILLNESS, AND WATER. TOGETHER THEY REPRESENT THE CYCLE OF LIFE AND DEATH.

A sleeping space should be harmonious and relaxing but capable of being invigorating in the morning as well as calming at night. The careful choice of color and use of space in the room will help achieve this.

SPACES

A panel of glass bricks above the bedhead allows light from the next door dressing room to come in but keeps the clothes and accessories stored in there out of view. The uncluttered space around the bed encourages the free flow of air and light.

Of all the rooms in the house, the bedroom is perhaps the most important place to achieve the right balance of yin and yang, so that the room is neither too energizing nor too soporific. The bedroom is also a place that has to accommodate a number of moods as it needs to be calming and relaxing, with the emphasis on yin to help you sleep. But, equally, it must have plenty of yang energy to make you wake up fresh, alert, and ready to face the day.

Create a yin-type atmosphere with a neutral background scheme and the addition of soft furnishings such as woollen throws, a neck roll or cushion, and curtains or heavy blinds. Choose the colors for these items from the warmer and richer end of the spectrum and ensure the lighting is subtle and soft. Although the pure Zen follower keeps their living and sleeping space as neat and orderly as possible, to further enhance the yin feeling of warmth and insularity of these areas, drape, pile, or layer the cushions and throws. For yang energy, the room also needs to be light and vital with invigorating, fresh colors and be kept neat and orderly. To achieve both these requirements in one room requires organization.

Use your curtains or blinds to influence the mood in a room and so the balance of yin and yang. When you wish to enhance the yin mood, close the curtains or use them to frame the edges of the window. Alternatively, if you favor blinds, keep them pulled down to full length or at least at half-mast to curb or restrict the flow of light. For times when yang energy is important, draw back the curtains to the outer edges of the window and roll or fold the blinds to the top to give maximum access to daylight. Also arrange cushions in a comfortable group for a relaxing yin environment and then line them up neatly and in an orderly way on the bed or seat to give a crisp, clean yang impression.

Wall-to-wall carpeting is soft and luxurious under bare feet in a bedroom but it is difficult to clean thoroughly, especially if it has a deep pile. Carpets with a high synthetic content may also encourage the development of static electricity. In addition, they tend toward the yin end of the spectrum. For something better balanced, think about installing a wood or similar smooth finish flooring, which may feel cool to the touch but it can be overlaid with rugs or mats around the bed area where naked feet first touch the floor. The mats can easily be shaken out of the window or thoroughly beaten in a back garden or yard and the floor easily brushed or wiped clean before they are replaced.

In many bedrooms there tends to be an abundance of parallel lines. Wardrobe doors, beds, closets and window frames are generally linear, so to achieve a suitable yin-yang balance, try to introduce some round shapes such as a circular mat, cushions, a globe lamp shade, or a disc mirror.

Use light and color, too, to maximize the yin-yang extremes. A dimmer switch on the main electrical lights will enable you, at just the slightest twist of a knob, to subdue or brighten the overall atmosphere of the room. Colors act differently in various strengths of light. For example, yellow is bright and zesty in daylight but by candlelight or soft lighting it appears golden, rich, and restful. Similarly, certain shades of blue and green can have a chameleon variation. Also bear in mind seasonal changes. What may appear warm and cozy in the winter might be hot and overpowering in the summer. This applies particularly to the hot colors such as red and orange, so choose your main colors with care.

RIGHT: The curved arms of the chair and two small, round mirrors on either side of the window help to counteract the many angular, straight lines of the bed and closets and help bring balance to the room.

Where possible, avoid having electrical equipment, other than basic lighting, in the bedroom. Electric currents can give a positive charge to ions in the air and bring an excess of energy into the room, which can be disturbing, especially at a time when the calmer yin qualities should be dominant. Electricity may also cause static reactions to occur, which can transmit a shock and be unpleasant. Place computers and other work-related items elsewhere. Work files and briefcases also act as reminders of work and consequently should not be stored in the room of rest either. In the same way, the television, mobile phone charger and hi-fi system may not be needed on a regular basis or could be used elsewhere, so keep the level of electrical charge in the air to a minimum.

Instead of running electric cables or wires under the bed, reduce the electrical field in this vulnerable area by running the cables along the skirting board or as far away as possible from the immediate vicinity of the bed. If cables do have to be run near the bed, make sure they are well secured to the wall or similar solid surface: loose wires can be dangerous.

RIGHT: The bed in the center of this room is "anchored" by a freestanding wall, behind which is the dressing and bathing area. If the bed was arranged on its own in the center of the room it would be isolated and vulnerable, but by being placed in front of the wall it has a purpose and a place.

ENHANCING SLEEP

Placing the bed in the right direction is a personal choice. Some people find that they sleep best with their head pointing toward the north and their feet to the south, but the structural confines of the room will play a major part in this decision. There are practical things to take into consideration, too. For example, for the sake of privacy, some people prefer to have their bed behind the door, so that when someone enters the room the bed is not the first thing they see.

The location of the window or windows is another factor. Few people find it restful to sleep with their head under the windowsill and their feet jutting into the room. Apart from the feeling of vulnerability there may also be drafts from an old or ill-fitting frame. Ideally, the bed should be opposite the window so that the morning light can fall on the pillow and if there is a view it can be enjoyed from the bed.

If a single bed has to be placed near a window, try to position it so that one side of the bed runs along the wall immediately under the window, and so that the head is in the protective join of the two corner walls. If this layout is planned for a double bed, consider how easy it will be for the person on the wall side of the bed to get in and out.

Mirrors are useful in a bedroom to look at your general appearance and for the application of make-up but they should be carefully positioned. It is thought to be unwise to have a mirror or any other decoration hanging directly above the pillow end of the bed. In purely practical terms, if the wire or string from which the article is hanging gives way it could land on your head. Also, in the realms of energy management, it is best to leave the area around the head free and uncluttered.

A mirror at the foot of the bed is also held to be inauspicious and is said by some to cause insomnia or difficulty with sleeping. Ideally, the mirror should be placed away from the bed and in front of a window so that the natural light will illuminate the face or body of the person being reflected, giving a clearer, brighter image. Alternatively, place a mirror used purely decoratively, opposite the window to enhance the incoming light and view.

In Japanese homes, the bed is generally low-level, most likely a futon on the tatami matting or a raised wooden plinth. For many Westerners a raised bed on legs or a divan base is preferable. A raised bed increases the flow of Chi and the air around the sleeping area and

The wall of windows at the foot of the bed provides not only a strong source of natural light but also a view. By waking and looking out of the window it will be easy to gauge the weather and keep in touch with the elements and nature. The blinds can be lowered and adjusted to give privacy and to obscure the view at night.

The featureless row of closets provide ample storage space yet do not intrude on the room. These types of door are often opened by pressing the opening edge, which releases a spring catch located within the closet, rather than using a knob or catch on the outside.

fibers and fabrics. Within a spring mattress there are pockets of air, which again help disperse sweat and heat; a solid foam mattress may only enhance the feelings of heat and damp. Foam pillows have a similar effect, but for asthma and allergy sufferers, feather or down pillows are best avoided and other more "breathable" and dust-free alternatives sought.

Good ventilation will also help a deep and restful night's sleep. A room that is too warm and dry causes dehydration, which will make you feel parched and lethargic when you wake. We are often tempted to sleep in a room that is too warm because, when first undressed, it feels comfortable, but the ideal room temperature is between 13 and 15°C (55 and 60°F) for healthy adults, but slightly warmer for babies and the elderly, who may not have such efficient circulation.

While good ventilation should be achieved, avoid drafts as these may cause stiffness and chills. By leaving a small upper window open or by putting a vent or similar outlet into a window or wall you will allow air to circulate throughout the day and night and prevent not only dryness and stuffiness, but also the build-up of stagnant Chi.

The noise factor can make it difficult to leave a window open. So if heavy traffic noise and fumes are going to disturb your slumbers try leaving the bedroom door ajar or bring a humidifier into the room. Try to avoid an electrically operated humidifier as it will introduce more electric current into the room. Instead, experiment with a simple bowl of water or a narrow water trough designed to hang on a radiator. If the room is not over-heated these may add sufficient moisture to make your sleeping environment comfortable.

In city apartments, double glazing and double doors or an enclosed lobby can help dampen exterior noise and distractions. Thick curtains or a combination of blinds and lined curtains can also muffle sounds that penetrate from the street. If temporary or unavoidable noise does become a problem then try playing some soothing or favorite music in the room. It is possible to dull exterior noise by masking it with a pleasant and regular sound in your immediate environment.

enables fluff and dust to be easily and effectively cleaned away. Many futon and bed mats are rolled up and stored in a closet when not in use, which also makes cleaning the floor area easy and effective.

The bedroom is a place where fine particles of dead skin are brushed off by the removal of clothes and the shaking of sheets. Hair that is shed in the night on a pillowcase or during brushing will also be deposited in these rooms more than anywhere else in the home, so thorough sweeping and vacuuming is important. The airing and turning of the mattress and duvet are also vital, not only for comfort but to prevent house mites and other organisms causing health problems. It is also recommended that a mattress should be renewed every ten years, not just from the point of view of freshness but also for support and posture reasons.

Where possible, use natural bedding materials. Linen and cotton are comfortable to sleep on and absorb the sweat and perspiration deposited during sleep. These natural fabrics are also durable and hard wearing as well as capable of being washed at high temperatures. A solid foam mattress and pillows are best replaced by natural, earthy

DEFINING SMALLER SPACES

In a studio room or a one room apartment where the bed is part of the main living area, try to segregate the space around the bed with a

LEFT: This spacious and uncluttered room has enough floor area to double as a meditation or exercise space. A mat could be unfurled and used without having to move any furniture, and then rolled and stored after use.

RIGHT: This platform bed is close to the traditional Zen-style sleeping arrangement, but as it overlooks a lower room and has no inner wall or screen it is really only suitable for a studio or single dwelling space.

screen or light curtain so that the other elements in the room do not interfere with or impinge on the area that has been designated for sleeping. To create a Zen-like space, the clutter and distractions of the rest of the room should be removed and the sleeping or meditation area isolated and kept pure.

In a one room setting, hide away electrical goods such as the television and computer in closets or mask them with a decorative throw or cloth when they are switched off. It is important to be able to remove yourself from a work environment so that you can have a definite time to yourself and your thoughts.

In a house where the bedroom is separate and the space sufficiently ample, there may be the opportunity to define small spaces within the bigger one. For example, it may be possible to allocate a specific area for exercise and another for reading, relaxing, or having an intimate chat with a close friend. If you do floor exercises and use a selection of hand weights or stretch bands, then these could be kept in a chest or covered box by an area of open floor space where they will most likely be used.

The requirements for a good night's sleep are relatively simple: a well padded futon or mattress and a cover. Where possible, electrical equipment should be kept to a minimum and as far away from the bed as possible. It is not advisable to have electrical cables running under the bed.

By placing a chair or sofa facing away from the bed you can form a small boudoir or sitting room where close friends or family can come and talk. If the sofa faces the bed you will focus the view on the most intimate part of the room, which you may find too personal, so switch the sofa around and put the back to the foot of the bed giving you a view of the rest of the room. A sofa or chair placed in the bedroom is ideal for solitary time spent in contemplation, relaxation, and calm.

If you follow Zen or similar meditative ideas, then a simple, uncluttered part of the room with a mat or cushion on which to sit, can be set aside purely for meditation. A small table or chest where incense can be stored or used, and a meditative object such as a single flower in a dish of water, could also be included.

If the room is large enough, consider sub-dividing it by building or installing a floating wall. This type of wall is built as a feature rather than for any practical supporting purpose; it is placed at a distance, away from the main wall of the room and is not generally fixed to the ceiling. If the wall is purely decorative then it can be made in a box shape from a lightweight material such as plywood and plastered to give it a more robust and permanent appearance. By placing this false wall some distance in from the real wall you create the illusion that the room is smaller and more intimate, without losing any of the practical space available.

A floating wall can double as a bedhead as well as a screen behind which a shower or row of built-in wardrobes or a dressing room can be created. Also use this type of fixture to give privacy to the bed area when a door opens directly onto it from a hallway. By placing the false wall in front of the door you can create a small lobby or vestibule as you enter and a safe haven beyond for the bed.

ORDER AND SPACE

Bedrooms are places that seem to invite clutter. Clothes that are left on a chair instead of hung up or put in a drawer, shoes that should be put away lurk singly or in pairs under the bed or the dressing table, and jewelry and cosmetics that you promise yourself are in regular use cover table tops and closets. Even the bedside table is prone to a build-up of tissue boxes, must-read novels, and magazines.

To achieve the sense of order and space that is important in Zen-style interiors, discipline and good storage are essential. The first stage is the edit by taking a long and honest look at the clothes and accessories you have. Try to identify what you really wear rather than things you hang on to in case you lose weight/it comes back in fashion/because you are emotionally attached to it. Set yourself a target, even pretend that you are going away for a year and you can only take one suitcase full of clothes for each season. Be honest and put what you don't need into storage bags for a thrift shop.

Once you have edited the contents of your wardrobe, you can set about making the best use of the space you have. By compartmentalizing various clothes and accessories and placing them in storage suited to their size you can actually create space. For example, by folding scarves and laying them flat in a drawer or clear plastic box you take up less room than hanging them in a closet or leaving them rolled up in a basket.

By making your bedroom a tidy and organized space to be in you will free up your mind and vision. This will make it easier for you to be calm and relaxed.

ZEN WATER

WATER HAS MANY SPIRITUAL AND REMEDIAL PROPERTIES AND IN SOME CULTURES SIGNIFIES CREATION AND REGENERATION. A NUMBER OF RELIGIONS ENCOURAGE THEIR FOLLOWERS TO BE IMMERSED OR BLESSED WITH WATER AS PART OF A CEREMONY. THE ACT OF BAPTISM REPRESENTS THE CLEANSING OF THE SOUL, THE "WASHING AWAY" OF THE PAST AND SO A NEW BEGINNING OR SPIRITUAL REBIRTH. IN ZEN PHILOSOPHY, RUNNING WATER CARRIES THE FORCE OF CHI ENERGY, WHICH SIGNIFIES VITALITY AND ENERGY. THE SOUND OF FLOWING WATER IS ALSO SAID TO BE CALMING AND CAPABLE OF WASHING AWAY TROUBLED THOUGHTS.

THE HEALTH-GIVING QUALITIES ATTRIBUTED TO WATER ARE WELL KNOWN. DRINKING WATER HELPS TO CLEANSE AND FLUSH THROUGH THE DIGESTIVE SYSTEM AND, AS OUR BODIES ARE MADE UP OF TWO-THIRDS WATER, IT IS IMPORTANT THAT THE FLUID LEVELS ARE KEPT CONSTANT AND REGULAR. AS WELL AS THE BENEFICIAL INTERNAL EFFECTS OF WATER, THE EXTERNAL ADVANTAGES ARE ALSO WORTH NOTING. SHOWERING AND RUBBING THE BODY WITH A LOOFAH OR COARSE CLOTH LOOSENS DEAD SKIN AND CLEANSES THE PORES, MAKING THE FACE AND BODY APPEAR FRESH AND VITAL. WASHING YOUR HAIR ALSO DISLODGES GRIME AND THE NATURAL SEBUM OR GREASE THAT IS SECRETED, LEAVING IT FRESH AND SHINY.

THE INVIGORATING EFFECT OF WASHING IS USEFUL FOR WAKING THE SYSTEM IN THE MORNING AND FOR REVIVING FLAGGING ENERGY LEVELS BEFORE GOING OUT BUT, IN THE EVENING OR AT TIMES OF RELAXATION, WALLOWING IN WATER IS ALSO CALMING AND SOOTHING.

This combined shower and bath is sufficiently large enough to do away with the restrictions of a shower cabinet and the unwelcome embraces of a damp plastic curtain.

ROOMS

Z

Stretching out in a bath of warm aromatic water can make you feel as though you are weightless, suspended in the liquid in which you lie. The heat also relaxes muscles and eases away tensions. Closing your eyes and letting the thoughts and worries in your mind dissolve will help you attain a Zen-like feeling of tranquility and calm.

BATHING AND WASHING

Bathing and washing usually take place in a bathroom and there are many ways of partaking in the process. Cold water, hot water, and steam are all integral parts of the cleansing ritual and they can be used in different ways—standing in a shower, lying in a bath, sitting with others in a sauna or having a quick splash over a hand basin. There are numerous styles of bath or water rooms and to find the one that suits you best analyze your needs and take an objective look at the space and budget you have.

E

There is a long history of bathing and bath building from the Greeks and Romans who indulged in communal baths as well as founding many of the well-known spa towns where the medicinal properties of the mineral salts found in the waters were used for healing as well as relaxing. Towns such as Bath in England and Spa, in eastern Belgium, from where the generic term for a watering place is derived, were both founded by the Romans.

The Japanese are regular bathers and unlike many Western cultures, where the bathroom is a very private place, many Eastern communities bathe in communal or family groups. The Japanese also scrub and cleanse their bodies in a shower or with a bucket of water before entering the bath, which is known as a *furo* and is designed to be used by more than one person and with water deep enough to cover the shoulders of a seated person.

Finns, Swedes, and other Scandinavian peoples enjoy the pleasure of a hot room or sauna. This is usually a wood-lined, air-tight cabin where water is poured over hot coals and often scented with birch bark or eucalyptus oil so that the cabin is filled with steam. The steam and heat cause the skin to sweat and cleanse the pores of impurities. When the cleansing process is over, the braver members of the sauna roll in the snow or hose themselves with ice-cold water to close the pores of their skin. Other hot rooms, such as the Turkish steam

N

A mirrored wall makes this bathroom appear twice the size it really is and the small mosaic tiles have been used to create an overall finish on the floor, the step, and the side of the bath, which adds to the impression of unity in the room.

LEFT: This curved glass surround contains the spray emitted by the shower but it is also a graceful and architectural feature. Being made of glass, the surround also appears light and is illuminated by the circular overhead window, which also echoes its curving shape.

RIGHT: Overhead windows can often be the perfect solution to getting natural light into a bathroom without giving up privacy.

room, have a wetter and more steamy atmosphere where people usually lie down on marble or stone slabs while engulfed in the misty water vapor.

All these communal forms of bathing or perspiring can be re-created in smaller sizes and installed in private homes for single or family use. Small-scale saunas and individual steam cabinets have been popular for some time and are especially enjoyed after playing sport. Another enjoyable bathing facility is the Jacuzzi, with jets of water that massage and pummel the muscles and skin.

WASHING OPTIONS

There are many specifically engineered baths that have automatic power jets or a cheaper and less permanent option is an aerated mat that can be fixed to the bath taps and will provide a similar if not as powerful effect. Massage is said to be good for the flow of blood around the body and it can also be beneficial in relaxing tense muscles, especially around the neck, shoulders, and scalp.

The rounded shape of this bath offsets the squareness of the stairs, the recessed ladder towel rail radiator and the recessed shelf beside the bath. The steps also provide easy access to the bath, making it easier to step down into from a mid rather than floor level.

requirement. There are also power showers that have extra pumps to increase the strength and volume of the water dispensed. Chi levels are enhanced by the shower's fast moving flow of water.

PLANNING THE LAYOUT

In the Zen-style bathroom, the decor should be simple, clean and functional. As it is the room where we are at our most vulnerable, stripped of clothing and any outer protection, it is a place where great care should be taken in the planning and layout so that the inhabitant can feel confident enough to relax in the intimate environment.

As in the bedroom, where dead skin and hair are also sloughed off the body, the bathroom needs to be a place where easy and effective cleaning can be carried out. The surfaces and coverings used in the bathroom should be wipeable and tolerant to cleaning agents and detergents. When planning the layout of the room try, where possible, to avoid difficult to reach areas such as the floor under an open-sided bath or a partially boxed-in lavatory where dust and fluff will accumulate but be tricky to extract.

Cold, sharp surfaces are probably the most unsettling elements in a bathroom, so where possible remove or reduce them to a minimum. The corners of a mirrored cabinet or an angular stool should be rounded or softened with protective caps or covers.

Heating is important in the bathroom, because after a warm bath you will feel the coldness of the air, but place pipes and radiators so that an unclothed body is not likely to be scorched or burnt by contact. Boxed in radiators or place those that double as towel rails sufficiently high up the wall and covered with towels to keep the hot bars out of harm's way.

Although steam can be beneficial to the body and skin, when it cools, it forms condensation, which can cause mold to grow on fabric, shower curtains, and the grouting between tiles. To clear the air and keep the dampness to a minimum, fit an extractor fan or air vent.

More traditional baths such as the classic roll top ceramic or reinforced plastic designs are also appropriate for the Zen-style bathroom. Their simple and practical forms and plain white finish make them unobtrusive and, with rounded edges, a restful and harmonious feature in the room.

For ease and speed, two hand basins can be useful for a couple. Instead of fighting for one basin to brush teeth and wash when you are dashing out of the door to get to work, two small basins, rather than one large and showy one, could ease tensions and make the morning exit more efficient and less stressful.

Site hand basins near a window or a good source of natural light and position a mirror over it with a light above. The mirror above a hand basin is where most close-up inspections of the face and hair take place so the light should be in plentiful supply.

Showers offer one of the most ecologically sound ways of washing as they use less water and energy than baths. The modern shower has an adjustable head that can vary the strength and impact of the water from soft and gentle to hard and needle-like, to suit your mood and

COVERING THE SURFACES

Cover walls with materials that can withstand the flow and adverse affects of water. Around the edges of the bath, shower area, and hand

RIGHT: Double basins are useful in a busy household where two adults may need to bathe and dress to leave for work at the same time. The simple water spouts plumbed through the wall also give unhindered access to the basin.

FAR RIGHT: The taps and faucet for this bath have been plumbed into a freestanding wall which means that the edge of the bath is clear and uncluttered. It also means that the surround of the bath can be simply and easily wiped down and the fittings washed or hosed down separately.

basin, ceramic tiles, a sheet of Plexiglas, polished steel, reinforced glass, or other similar material will withstand splashes and steam. In other areas where steam and condensation are more prevalent, a good latex or similar paint finish will be sufficient.

Flooring is important, too, because it needs to be easy to wipe and clean, and it should be water-resistant but comfortable underfoot. Natural materials are again most Zen-like but impregnate materials such as cork and wood with a water-resilient finish for protection, otherwise water may seep in and make it swell and split.

Cork for flooring or wall covering is usually sold in rolls or pre-cut tiles and comes in a natural, warm brown color (dyed and colored corks are available). It comes from the outer bark of the cork oak or *Quercus suber* and is a renewable resource because the tree replaces the bark it loses. Cork is hard wearing and a good insulator against cold and noise and has a soft cushion-like feel underfoot.

Some woods such as cedar and cypress have aromatic properties, which can add to the pleasure of bathing and may be used in the construction of a bath or enclosure. When the wood becomes warm

and damp it may release a perfume. If you want to install a wooden tub like those favored by the Japanese, choose carefully as some need to be kept constantly damp, otherwise the sides can dry out and crack, which may cause leaking. Teak is a wood favored by many for a wooden tub because it has more natural oil than other woods and its color will not fade or become dull with constant exposure to water.

Other natural flooring materials such as slate or terracotta tiles can be cold and hard underfoot, although waterproof and practical. To overcome the chilly difficulties, you could install under-floor heating, which would make tiles and even concrete floors warm and comfortable to walk on barefoot. To counteract the hardness of the surface, position flat woven cotton rugs or wooden deck-style grids where the bather is most likely to stand and linger.

ENHANCING LIGHT AND SPACE

Creating the right mood and atmosphere in the bathroom is useful in achieving a Zen-like state of relaxation of tranquility. As in the

Z
E
N

WATER ROOMS

The rounded shape of these simple bowl-like basins is echoed in the uplighter and the unusual rounded edge of the mirrors that hang above each basin.

There are few signs of plumbing pipes or fittings around this basin, which has the simple and uncluttered line of an old-fashioned bowl on a wooden shelf. Its simplicity and function are married to create a pleasing and Zen-like appearance.

bedroom, lighting can be a great help when it comes to altering the mood. The lighting will need to be strong and well-focused over the hand basin for applying cosmetics or shaving, but may be dimmed or turned off and replaced by scented candles for an intimate and calming evening bath.

Position any candles carefully so they do not come into direct contact with the skin, towels, or paper, which may scorch or catch fire. Also place any lighted object such as a candle or incense stick on a dish or stand so that dripping wax or ash will not damage any wood or polished surface.

Electricity and water is a dangerous combination so enclose lights within a cover or shade and place switches outside the room. Only fit a power point for an electric shaver if it has specific safety recommendations and also ground metal baths and pipes to make them safe. Also on a safety note, avoid having glass or other breakable ornaments in the bathroom and ensure that any glass present, such as in shower cabinet enclosures, shelves, or a mirror over the hand basin, are reinforced or have a recognized seal of safety.

Where possible, allow daylight to penetrate the bathroom, although this can be difficult to combine with adequate privacy. Sandblasted or opaque windows will preserve modesty and still allow light through, and if the windows are sufficiently high, only the lower section need be screened. Overhead windows or skylights can be a good alternative way of bringing natural light in, and may also provide a porthole-like view of clouds, sky, tree tops and birds without the danger of being looked in on.

To create a Zen-like water or bathroom you should try to achieve a feeling of space. When you are naked, free of clothes and the trappings of everyday life, the sensation of liberation can only be enhanced by a simple and clutter-free environment. Adequate and well-placed storage is necessary to maximize the space available. Keep items such as towels, cosmetics, bath preparations, and scented candles neatly out of the way in closets under the hand basin or in a row of fitted closets. Medicines and other potentially noxious substances such as cleaning agents and detergents should be kept out of children's reach and under lock and key.

If there is ample space in the bathroom think about creating an area for rest and repose within the privacy of this intimate space. A chaise longue or bench covered with a futon or cushion can be the perfect place on which to stretch out and cool down after a bath, as well as a place to muse on the events of the day.

This area may also be used to comfortably undertake part of a beauty routine such as the application of a face mask or a manicure, or for exercise such as yoga or calisthenics. Strength and movement are two important physical aspects of Zen and are practiced through exercises such as kung fu or t'ai chi, which can lead to a meditative state. In *The Complete Book of Zen* by Wong Kiew Kit, the benefits of exercise linked with meditation are explained like this, "When a one-pointed mind is attained in the process of practicing a kung fu set, some practitioners may experience a Zen awakening or satori during the final standing meditation."

If you have a large bathroom, you may also decide to incorporate exercise equipment such as a step machine and stationary bicycle. Keep these as far away from the bath and shower area as possible so that they are not affected by the heat and steam. Having an exercise area in the same room as the shower or bath means that the sweat of the exertions can be quickly and easily washed away without having to move from one room to another or from one temperature to another.

ACHIEVING TRANQUILITY

To achieve tranquility in the water or bathroom, keep the surroundings safe, warm, uncluttered, and calm. This environment can be further enhanced by subtle scents and aromas and a wrap or towel covering that is comfortable and enveloping. If there is a view or something pleasant to concentrate on, a state of relaxation and contemplation should be easily attained.

As well as scented candles, perfume the air with bath additives such as salts, oils, and crystals. Bath salts enriched with minerals, like those found in the spa towns favored by the Romans and later by the social classes in the eighteenth century, should be well dissolved in the water to prevent a gritty or sand-like roughness forming in the bottom of the bath. Oils can be used in a shower as well as a bath and should be applied all over the body with a moist sponge before being rinsed off. Many natural ingredients provide mood enhancing aromas, too. For example, lavender and rose are said to be calming while citrus-based products with lime, lemon, and orange zest will invigorate and waken-up the system.

To enhance the yin qualities of a perfumed soak, make sure you have a set of thick-pile or velvet-cotton towels in a large size like a blanket, to be used as a warm and comforting wrap. However, you will also need some fine, waffle-textured linen towels stored in a closet as these provide the perfect yang-like invigorating scrub down after a bracing, morning shower.

Some plants thrive in the moist warm atmosphere of a bathroom, and in keeping with Zen principles having a plant in the water room will introduce an element of nature. In particular, the soft shapes and forms of ferns help to redress the balance of linear and angular shapes. Some orchids also enjoy the humidity of a bathroom, and the beauty of the flowers and the graceful arch of the leaves can be a soothing and meditative focal point.

This combined bath and shower room makes use of natural materials and simple forms. Stone and wood are used to create the bathing area and the shower attachments are plumbed through a stone clad wall.

OBJECTS

WHILE ZEN PHILOSOPHY TEACHES THAT ONE'S POSSESSIONS ARE ONE'S BURDENS, THE ART AND POETRY OF ZEN EXTOL THE EXQUISITENESS OF NATURE AND THE JOY THAT CAN BE RECEIVED FROM STUDYING AND CONTEMPLATING A THING OF BEAUTY. A FEW WELL-CHOSEN AND CLEVERLY DISPLAYED OBJECTS CAN SPEAK VOLUMES, WHILE A GREAT MUDDLE OF THIS AND THAT, HEAPED RATHER THAN ARRANGED, MAY BE LIKE AN INCOMPREHENSIBLE BABBLE. THE EDITING PROCESS IS ABOUT TRAINING THE MIND AND EYE TO APPRECIATE AND IDENTIFY WHAT HAS REAL SUBSTANCE AND VALUE. BY ANALYZING WHAT IT IS ABOUT AN OBJECT THAT APPEALS TO YOU, YOU WILL GET TO KNOW YOUR OWN TASTES AND ULTIMATELY FIND OUT MORE ABOUT YOURSELF AND WHAT GIVES YOU PLEASURE.

WITH THE CLEAN, PLAIN DECOR THAT IS TYPICAL OF A ZEN-INSPIRED ROOM, THE EYES ARE DRAWN TO DETAIL THAT THEY MIGHT ONCE HAVE OVERLOOKED. WHEN THERE IS A FEAST FOR THE EYES TO STUDY AND THE MIND TO APPRECIATE, THERE IS A TENDENCY TO SKIP QUICKLY FROM ONE THING TO ANOTHER, TAKING IN A LITTLE ABOUT A LOT OF THINGS. BUT GIVEN ONE SINGLE ITEM TO EXPLORE, THE EYES AND MIND WILL STUDY IN DEPTH AND FIND ANGLES AND NUANCES THAT MAY HAVE BEEN OVERLOOKED BEFORE TAKING A CLOSER LOOK.

OBJECTS NEED NOT BE EXPENSIVE OR ELABORATE TO BE BEAUTIFUL OR WORTHY OF CONTEMPLATION. ORDINARY, EVERYDAY THINGS CAN HAVE AN INTRINSIC BEAUTY. AT FIRST IT MAY NOT BE OBVIOUS, BUT AFTER A LITTLE CONTEMPLATION AND STUDY, THE HIDDEN TREASURE OR ASPECT MAY REVEAL ITSELF. THESE SIMPLE OBJECTS CAN BE DISPLAYED IN DIFFERENT WAYS TO HIGHLIGHT VARIOUS ASPECTS OF THEIR APPEARANCE.

Right: Ordinary, everyday objects can be attractive. A wicker tray, a hand-made jug and a bowl can be as decorative and pleasing as any number of fancy and colorful items.

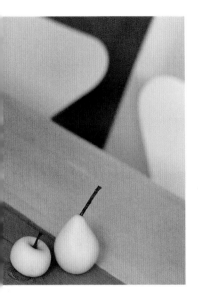

Above: Simple, natural shapes are immortalized and preserved in white china. Without their natural color it is the form and shape of the fruit that become the subject of admiration.

& ORNAMENTS

Z

E

N

LEFT: The recess around this fireplace creates a simple but effective frame to the black square. Inside the square, the fire—or in this case the candles—becomes a focal point.

ABOVE: The balance of objects on display is important, but balance may be achieved by odd numbers rather than even and by pyramid shapes rather than squares. Here the two paintings in the center of the cabinet create a pyramid shape above the three panels of the doors.

A simple, rounded stone picked up from a beach or river bank or a bleached piece of driftwood may bring back memories of the time and place where it was found and of the landscape and setting to which it belonged. Not only is an object like this attractive to look at, it has the added appeal of its texture. Stones can be displayed alone or in a group, dry or brought to life in a glass dish of water.

An empty, dark fireplace is initially a blank and uninspiring chasm, yet it can act as a border or frame for a deeper picture. A few glowing embers or a pile of ash may lead your eye to the burned layers of wood or the strata of coal, once rock, that is now just a shadow of its former self. When the fire is out and the ashes cleared, place a small group of candles in the dark recess and light them to create a focal point and animated element in the blackness.

Nature is full of attractive and intriguing things and seasonal changes also help to keep you in tune with nature and passing time. For example, a single, fresh green leaf with its network of sap-carrying veins that run along the underside, transporting nutrients to the furthest point (as our own veins carry blood throughout the human body), looks vital and vibrant. The same leaf, a few weeks later, dead and dried reveals in fine detail the skeletal form of the once living network, still a thing of beauty and fascination.

A spider's web is another work of art, the intricate weaving of the finest threads for a deadly purpose. Glistening with dew drops in the early morning it appears jewel-like and deceptively vulnerable. But an object like this cannot be harvested and brought indoors, it must be appreciated from a window or doorway or photographed during a stroll through the countryside, and framed for future viewing.

Domestic trappings can also create their own magic. The shadow cast around a small table lamp creates an area of shade and mystery and may make an object appear to stand out from the background. Furthermore, the pool of light will highlight the grain of wood on the table on which it stands or the folds of the newspaper or pages of the book that lie beneath.

MARRYING FORM AND FUNCTION

Zen also appreciates the marriage of form and function; the harmony achieved by an object that serves its purpose well but is also pleasing to the eye. With the belief that less is more, each item selected for use in the home should be not only useful but also attractive. For example, look at a chair that displays a balance of color, weight and structure, or a bowl or jug with a shapely handle or foot and a mottled or unusual glaze. The object itself is still utilitarian, but it has an edge, something that makes it more than just useful.

Likewise, hand-thrown rather than commercially produced pottery can be admired for its special features. A hand-made vessel carries something of the character of its maker, it may also be irregular with an unusual glaze or finish and as it is hand-made, it is a unique and unrepeatable piece, which gives it an exceptional quality.

The art of calligraphy is also an important part of Zen life and is often applied to a few well-chosen words or symbols deftly assigned with a brush and ink to a scroll or paper. The words are often a thought to dwell on or else a message or dictum to be remembered. A typical haiku or Zen poem has seventeen syllables in a five, seven, five configuration. The example that follows, which is a translation of a haiku by Basho, a Japanese poet of the seventeenth century, shows

The bright colors of these simple bowls, in contrast with the stark white glass table and white walls, are a perfect example of how functional objects can also become decorative when they are carefully positioned in a room.

how a few words can readily conjure up a picture, a reminiscence and an idea for further thought.

> "Ah! the old pond
> A frog jumps in
> The water's sound."

The actual texture and shape of the calligraphy letters or symbols formed with a brush may also provide something for the eye to linger on. There will be areas where the ink is heavy and dark, and others where it is lighter and less concentrated; points where the brush has been lifted deftly and neatly to form a crisp point, and others where the finish is softer and more fluid.

A more commercial form of decoration is the Zen sand garden, sold in kit form in shops and stores. This simple garden is a small, lip-edged tray filled with fine sand and a fork-size wooden rake. The idea is that by raking the sand you create patterns, and through doing this creative and calming act you concentrate the mind. The Zen garden has

OBJECTS & ORNAMENTS

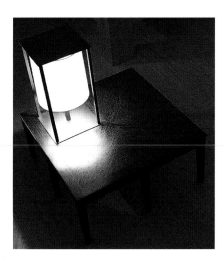

LEFT: The arrangement of these simple Shaker baskets makes them appealing—the graduation of sizes draws the eye to the details of the small raised feet and the fine, square-edged handles.

ABOVE LEFT: By positioning this light on the edge of the table the squareness of the shade takes on the appearance of the corner that it conceals.

ABOVE: The clean lines of this chair are attractive and the details of the continuation of the arms as a feature across the back stands out against the pale upholstery.

become an executive toy, along with the clacking metal balls of the Newton's Cradle, but it has its roots in the therapeutic, relaxing, and meditative ways that are a part of the Zen philosophy of life.

CHOOSING AND ARRANGING ORNAMENTS

As Zen has a multi-cultural history spreading from India to China, Japan and then to the West there are no specific objects that must be displayed. For a lay Zen person, an object should be something that calms and concentrates the mind rather than a symbol or token depicting something that is beyond comprehension or too complex to meditate on easily.

Some people find that the simple act of burning an incense cone or stick offers a two-fold point of interest. The burning incense not only provides a soothing, olfactory pleasure but by watching the curls of smoke rise and disperse, the eye and mind are also engaged. The smoke appears to be a living and moving thing that travels into the distance until it finally disappears.

Organize and group objects to show them in their best light or to highlight their different qualities. The grouping of uneven numbers of items creates interest as does the juxtaposition of shapes and textures, smooth by rough, open by solid. The rough and textured piece of driftwood next to the smooth roundness of a pebble, the solid regularity of a pottery bowl next to the open wickerwork of a tray, or the ethereal, paper-like leaves of a bunch of flowers next to the solid squareness of a fireplace or bookcase are but a few combinations.

Varying the height of things in a group can also create a picture. For example, a couple of tall bottles arranged with a few mid-height jars and some cups or small bowls at a lower level will give the impression of depth to the arrangement because the eye is drawn inward and upward through the group.

Playing shapes off against each other is also an interesting ploy. The arrangement of two oblong framed pictures hung above a side cabinet with three square doors would be one way of doing this. Think again of the odd number grouping theory—the two pictures create a

pyramid shape above the closet doors, which draws the eyes upward. If there were three pictures lined directly above each of the doors the arrangement would be parallel and even, which would be predictable and so less eye-catching.

USING COLOR TO ENHANCE DISPLAYS

Mount and frame pictures and photographs as simply as possible so that the subject of the artwork can be seen in full rather than lost in a complicated and colorful arrangement of mounts or hidden behind the ornate carvings of a heavy gilded frame. In some cases, a contrasting mount can emphasize the picture or photograph, but try to keep within the same family of colors. For example, if you are framing a print that has been put onto a cream paper, look for a mount in a darker shade of that color or in one of the colors used in the print itself. Using colors from the same family will add to the harmony of the finished piece.

The use of shades of the same color can also be applied to cloths, mats, and banners. When an object is placed on or against a contrasting piece of fabric, it is given a special emphasis as it is framed much as a print or photograph is by a mount. Fabric banners and mats are useful because they can be easily changed not only for cleaning but also for a change in mood or if the object is replaced. A simple banner of a single colored or self-patterned fabric laid as a strip down the center of a table will protect the surface and will also create a backdrop to a vase of flowers or a group of objects placed on it.

A group of white china fruits would look almost invisible on a limewashed or white painted table, but by placing them on an oatmeal colored, natural jute runner they stand out yet are still in harmony with the table. Banners can also be hung on walls or use them in a plain white room to create a distinguishing background for a shapely chair or an arrangement of leaves in a vase.

These glass items take on a whole new dimension when placed in front of a window or light source. The translucent quality of the material become obvious when light plays on it and the color becomes more intense.

OBJECTS & ORNAMENTS

ZEN

By varying the height of objects in a group you can create an interesting composition. Again, simple everyday objects but with similar finishes and colors can be arranged in attractive ways.

147

WAY OUT

THE RELATIONSHIP BETWEEN HUMANS AND NATURE IS MUCH DISCUSSED IN ZEN. IDEALLY, WE SHOULD BE CONSTANTLY IN TOUCH WITH OUR OUTDOOR SURROUNDINGS, THE CHANGING FACE OF NATURE AND THE SIMPLE PLEASURES AND EXPERIENCES PROVIDED BY THE WIND, SUN, AND RAIN. THIS IS NOT AN EASY TASK FOR CITY DWELLERS OR THOSE WITH A BUSY WORKING SCHEDULE, BUT THERE ARE WAYS IN WHICH YOU CAN BRING NATURE CLOSER TO YOU SO THAT IT IS A PART OF YOUR EVERYDAY LIFE RATHER THAN SOMETHING THAT YOU HAVE TO GO AND SEARCH FOR.

THERE ARE LARGE AND SMALL SCALE PROJECTS THAT CAN BE IMPLEMENTED TO CREATE A CLOSER CONTACT WITH NATURE. YOU CAN LANDSCAPE AND PLANT AN EXISTING GARDEN TO CONFORM TO THE ASIAN STYLE OR FORM A SMALL ZEN GARDEN WITHIN AN EXISTING GARDEN. A ROOF TERRACE OR CONSERVATORY EXTENSION WILL TAKE A HOUSE OR APARTMENT OUT TO THE GARDEN AND BRING THE GARDEN INTO THE HOUSE, GIVING A CLOSER AND MORE REGULAR LINK WITH THE GREAT OUTDOORS.

A CONSERVATORY WITH GLASS WALLS AND CEILING IS ALSO AN IDEAL PLACE TO PLANT AND GROW YOUR OWN GREENERY. OR, FOR THOSE WHO DO NOT HAVE THE TIME OR INCLINATION TO TEND PLANTS, THE CONSERVATORY PROVIDES A WAY OF SITTING AMONG NATURE AND EXPERIENCING THE CHANGING WEATHER WITHOUT HAVING TO WATER, WEED, OR WRAP UP IN AN OVERCOAT. HOWEVER, REMEMBER THAT ALTHOUGH PERFECT IN SPRING AND AUTUMN, THEY CAN BECOME UNBEARABLY HOT DURING THE HEIGHT OF THE SUMMER SO ENSURE YOU HAVE EFFICIENT VENTILATION AND ERECT SOME FORM OF SCREEN OR CANOPY.

The longitudinal lines of the planks on this decking make the outdoor space appear to be long and the lines draw the eye along them to the furthest point of the garden. The awning echoes the lines and adds to the feeling of length and distance in what is essentially a confined space.

& BEYOND

Furniture may also need to be covered to prevent the sun fading or damaging upholstery. Simple calico or rush blinds are sympathetic to the surroundings and can be arranged so they are drawn back to the outer edges of the room or walls when not in use. Attach lightweight canvas or calico blinds with high-tension wire on yachting cleats to create an airy and billowing appearance.

The Zen garden is designed to be a place of escape from the demands of daily work, noise, and chaos. It is a place of solitude and relaxation as well as a place where the body and spirit can be close to nature. Although it may be difficult to cut off all exterior noise—cars, airplanes, ringing phones, and honking horns—you may be able to create a screen or barrier. The barrier can be used to distance the annoyances and focus your interest, both visual and aural, within the garden so that your senses are pleased by what is immediate to them rather than distracted by what is beyond.

PLANTING A ZEN GARDEN

The elements of wind and water and the harmony of shapes and foliage are used to create balance so the foliage or greenery should be carefully selected to give the right effect. Choose plants of different heights. Plant tall bamboos or gracefully cascading willow trees toward the back or in a clump as a special feature. Mid-height shrubs and bushes, especially ones that can be pruned and trimmed to limit their growth, will make a mid-height level and below that plant a range of small plants. Ground cover, whether bark chips, tiny stones or a rapidly spreading carpet plant will give yet another dimension. When designing these planting schemes, check that the plants you are hoping to grow at lower levels are especially suited to a darker and more moist environment.

As most plants in this style of garden are leafy, select the color and shape carefully. Ensure there is a good balance of fine spidery leaves with large, solid leaves, and light grays and soft yellows mixed with richer, dark green tones. Finally, taking the balance of planting to its most refined, make sure there are areas of light and shade, the yin and yang of the garden.

Choose plants for a Zen garden with long-term growth in mind. Longevity and links with the environment are important to the spirit

LEFT: Simple sculptural shapes and screens can create private and quiet areas within a large garden. This plain curved wall gives the impression of being surrounded and secure.

LEFT: If you don't have a garden, try to find a window or part of a room where you can create the feeling or experience of being outdoors. Even if you do have a garden, you might like to do this for days when the weather prohibits sitting outdoors.

of the garden so plants that you might wish to move around, for example when they are in bloom or if they need to be moved from direct sunlight, should be planted in portable containers rather than dug up and replanted.

INTRODUCING GARDEN FEATURES

Garden features rather than flowers are the important part of a Zen garden. The layout is more about the balance of yin and yang, the life-giving forces of nature and texture and harmony than beds of bright flowers. Originally, the tea garden or *cha-nima*, associated with the tea house and the tea drinking ritual, formed the basis of what is now referred to as the Zen garden.

There are three main decorative features that should be introduced if possible. The first is the *tsukubai* or water basin, a simple rounded stone with a recess or dip filled with water. Beside the stone there is a ladle, generally made from cedar, which is used to scoop the water up so that the hands and face can be washed before entering the tea

house. This ritual cleansing has deep religious significance and stems from the belief that true and natural beauty cannot be seen if it is concealed by impurities.

The second feature is the *ishidoro* or stone lantern. This squat, carved house-shaped lantern is often raised on a plinth and is a symbol of a guiding light along life's pathway. It is also a practical object that can be used to illuminate a corner of a garden in the evening or for concealing insect repellent candles such as citronella, which will not harm the insects but will provide some safety from their bites. The carved stone lantern can also be a focus for offerings of flowers or incense or as a temple or shrine.

The third feature so often seen in a Zen garden is stepping stones. Once again, these can have a practical function in that they can be positioned to form a pathway across a wet lawn or muddy area as well as being aesthetically pleasing. The stones are usually created from large, rounded boulders and may be placed symbolically, where they are visually pleasing or work with the shape and flow of the garden's natural shape.

Z

E

N

This terrace acts as a barrier between the outer and inner worlds. It is a threshold, like the area immediately inside the front door. The platform is a neutral place where elements of both worlds can be enjoyed.

RIGHT: This decking acts like a bridge over a sea of stones. It links one part of the house to another and may be used to form a barrier between the outer, more commonly used areas and the inner, more private world.

Although not as important as the first three elements, a pathway is another traditional feature of this style of garden. The path, which may be paved with wood or stone, should lead to the tea house or, in Western gardens, to an arbor or area of solitude. The pathway is also a clear channel along which the energy of Chi may pass.

The stepping stones and stone pathway need not be the only areas where rocks are used. Pebbles are often seen in Asian gardens not only for their pleasing shape and color but also because they are good for drainage. A narrow path of stones around the edge of a building makes an attractive and practical feature. Stones do not absorb or hold the water like grass or clay so the area around which they are laid will remain dry and clear. It is also easier to weed and maintain an area of rocks close to a building.

Because of their good drainage properties, pebbles can also be set in a pattern as a base for a fountain or water feature. Water running over the rocks creates a lively and appealing bubbling and splashing effect, which is also good Chi. In addition, pile the pebbles up to form a raised point or feature in an area of flatness.

In other places where stone or grass are not appropriate coverings, wooden decking is a sympathetic, natural alternative. Lay the decking with a slight gap between the planks so that water can drain away and treat the wood to ensure it will withstand the effects of wind and rain. Unless you specifically want the wood to weather and fade, which can give it a more natural appearance, check that the preservative finish is also sun-resistant.

CREATING AN INDOOR GARDEN

If you do not have access to a garden, or an area where you can make one, there are ways of creating a Way Out, within. The simplest way is to bring bamboo or similar plants into your home, but you can also create areas where outdoor elements are emphasized.

In Japanese gardens where a pond or other water feature it is not possible, stone, gravel or sand is laid to represent water in a style known as *kare sansui*. Replicate this in miniature on a tray or trough on a balcony or even in an area set aside for an indoor garden. The base of this miniature *kare sansui* garden can be simply a sheet of heavyweight plastic or a rimmed palette, which contains the sand and stone. If using plastic sheeting, make sure there are a few drainage holes so that it won't become waterlogged with rain if left outside. Lay a level layer of sand across the bottom of the container and bed in the stones; if they are rounded pebbles, lay them pointing in the same direction so that they appear to "flow." Embed broken pieces of slate at an angle in the sand so that they appear to lap, like waves.

Alternatively, make a trellis screen into a "living" wall by growing ivy or similar indoor plants along it. Wind chimes placed by an open window will tinkle with the movement of the air, and the tempo of their music will inform you of the strength and speed of the wind, without having to look outside.

There are numerous inexpensive and simple ways of creating a closer link with nature, and bringing the outside into your home or taking the inside out. Water plants and bulbs that grow in a glass container with their roots spreading down and the green leaves and flowers gradually appearing, are one such way of keeping in touch, and even if you don't have an open fire, a basket of logs or a large vase of twigs will bring an earthy element into a room.

LEFT: Glass rooms are a perfect way of keeping in touch with nature and the elements without having to be exposed to them. You can enjoy the sun and color of the spring before the temperature rises and the mellowness of the autumn without the accompanying chill.

ABOVE: This glass extension brings the outside in as it is used for growing plants as well as an area to enjoy the pleasures of the garden. Its double-storey height means that the heat generated under the glass and the scents of the flowers can also be experienced indoors.

INDEX

Page numbers in **bold** represent photographs

ACKNOWLEDGMENTS

1 View/Peter Cook; 2 Arcaid/Richard Bryant/Architects Pawson & Silvestrin; 6 Ray Main/Mainstream/Architect Brian Ma-Siy; 8-9 Arcaid/Richard Bryant/ table designed by John Pawson; 12 Elizabeth Whiting & Associates/Tim Street-Porter/designer Brian Murphy; 14 The Interior Archive/Andrew Wood; 15 Ray Main/Mainstream/Architect Gregory Phillips; 16 Paul Ryan/ International Interiors/designers Haskins & Page; 17 Elizabeth Whiting & Associates/Andreas von Einsiedel/designer Clare Bataille; 18 View/Dennis Gilbert/Rick Mather Architects; 21 Narratives/Jan Baldwin; 22 Paul Ryan/International Interiors/Architects Hariri & Hariri; 23 Marie Claire Maison/Marie-Pierre Morel/Daniel Rozensztroch; 25 The Interior Archive/Henry Wilson; 26 Sidnome Petrone Gartner Architects/Jeff McNamara; 27 Arcaid/Rodney Weidland; 28 View/Peter Cook/Architects Sergison Bates; 29 Narratives/Jan Baldwin/ceramics designer Hylton Nel; 31 Elizabeth Whiting & Associates/Tom Leighton; 32 Ray Main/Mainstream; 33 Ray Main/Mainstream/designer Kelly Hoppen; 34 Arcaid/Earl Carter/Belle/Synam Justin Bialek Architects; 35 Elizabeth Whiting & Associates/Michael Faulkner and Lynn McGregor; 36 Arcaid/Richard Bryant/Rick Mather Architects; 38 Ray Main/Mainstream/Architect Susanna Lumsden; 39 The Interior Archive/Edwina van der Wyck; 41 The Interior Archive/Henry Wilson; 42 Ray Main/Mainstream/Architect Chris Cowper; 43 Marie Claire Maison/Gilles de Chabaneix/Catherine Ardouin; 45 Paul Ryan/International Interiors/designer Jacqueline Morabito; 46 Arcaid/Richard Bryant/Architects Paxton Locher; 48 above Paul Ryan/International Interiors/designer Jacqueline Morabito; 48 below Paul Ryan/International Interiors/designer Jacqueline Morabito; 49 Elizabeth Whiting & Associates/ Jean-Paul Bonhommet; 50-51 The Interior Archive/Fritz von der Schulenburg; 52 View/Chris Gascoigne; 54-55 Ray Main/Mainstream/designed by Vicente Wolf of Vicente Wolf Associates Inc.; 57 Ray Main/Mainstream; 58 The Interior Archive/Fritz von der Schulenburg; 59 Ray Main/Mainstream/ designer Drew Plunkett; 61 View/Peter Cook; 62 Arcaid/Richard Bryant/Architects Pawson & Silvestrin/Warren & Victoria Miro; 63 Ray Main/Mainstream/ designer Nick Allan; 64 View/Peter Cook; 66 Eric Morin/Kenzo; 67 The Interior Archive/Fritz von der Schulenburg; 70 Arcaid/Richard Bryant/architects Pawson & Silvestrin; 73 Sidnome Petrone Gartner Architects/ Langdon Clay; 74 Ray Main/Mainstream/designer Drew Plunkett; 76 Arcaid/ Richard Bryant/Architects Pawson & Silvestrin; 77 Arcaid/Richard Bryant/ Architects Pawson & Silvestrin; 79 Ray Main/Mainstream/Architect Mark Guard; 80 Paul Ryan/International Interiors/designer Charles Rutherfoord; 81 The Interior Archive/Simon Upton; 82 Marie Claire Maison/Ingalill Snitt/Catherine Ardouin; 83 View/Chris Gascoigne; 84-85 Paul Ryan/International Interiors/architect David Ling; 87 Elizabeth Whiting & Associates/Michael Crockett/designers Munkenbeck & Marshall; 88 Richard Glover/Architect Sophie Hicks; 89 Ray Main/Mainstream/Architect Chris Cowper; 90-91 Elizabeth Whiting & Associates/Tim Street-Porter/designer Eve Steele; 92 Ray Main/Mainstream/ Architect John Pawson; 93 Arcaid/Richard Bryant/Seth Stein Architects; 95 Ray Main/Mainstream/Architect Stephen Featherstone; 96 The Interior Archive/Fritz von der Schulenburg; 98-99 Richard Glover; 100 Ray Main/ Mainstream/Architect Spencer Fung; 101 Marie Claire Maison/Gilles de Chabaneix/Marie Kalt; 103 Arcaid/Richard Bryant/Architect Seth Stein; 104 Ray Main/Mainstream; 106 The Interior Archive/Fritz von der Schulenburg; 107 Ray Main/Mainstream/Architect Chris Cowper; 108-109 Arcaid/Richard Bryant/Architects Paxton Locher; 111 Ray Main/Mainstream/Architect Spencer Fung; 112 Ray Main/Mainstream/Architect Stephen Featherstone; 114 The Interior Archive/Herbert Ypma; 115 The Interior Archive/Fritz von der Schulenburg; 116-117 Arcaid/Richard Bryant/Paxton Locher Architects; 118 The Interior Archive/Andrew Wood; 120 Paul Ryan/International Interiors/designer Gordon & de Vries; 121 Marie Claire Maison/Gilles de Chabaneix/Catherine Ardouin; 122 Ray Main/Mainstream/designer Drew Plunkett; 125 Elizabeth Whiting & Associates; 126-127 Paul Ryan/International Interiors/architect David Ling; 128 Marie Claire Maison/Nicolas Tosi; 129 Ray Main/Mainstream/designer Nick Allan; 130 View/Chris Gascoigne/Seth Stein Architects; 132 The Interior Archive/Andrew Wood; 133 Narratives/Jan Baldwin; 134 Paul Ryan/International Interiors/designer Paul Pasman; 135 Paul Ryan/ International Interiors/designer Jacqueline Morabito; 137 Arcaid/Richard Bryant/Architects Pawson & Silvestrin; 138 Ray Main/Mainstream/designer Kelly Hoppen; 139 Narratives/Jan Baldwin; 140 Ray Main/Mainstream/ Architect Mark Guard; 141 Ligne Roset; 143 Ray Main/Mainstream/Architect Mark Guard; 144 Paul Ryan/International Interiors; 145 left Arcaid/Earl Carter/Belle/designer Christian Liaigre; 145 right Ligne Roset; 146 Elizabeth Whiting & Associates/Helen Guinness; 147 Arcaid/Trevor Mein/Belle; 148 The Interior Archive/Fritz von der Schulenburg; 150-151 Arcaid/Richard Bryant/Rick Mather Architects; 152 Elizabeth Whiting & Associates/Tim Street-Porter/designer Moore, Ruble Yudell; 153 The Interior Archive/Fritz von der Schulenburg; 154 Sidnome Petrone Gartner Architects/Langdon Clay; 155 Arcaid/Richard Bryant/Paxton Locher Architects; 156 View/Dennis Gilbert/Rick Mather Architects; 157 View/Dennis Gilbert.